Dance with the Elephants

The Ultimate Guide to Transform Your Small Business into Big Profits

Philip I Walker

ISBN: 1494793830

ISBN-13: 978-1494793838

This book is dedicated to CGB, for causing me to change my world view. For helping me, with ruthless compassion, to choose insights into possibility over insights into veracity, and to adopt curiosity over judgement. It may have taken me over ten years to understand just how good a teacher you were for me, but I got there in the end. 'Come to the edge', you said. When I came, you pushed me and I flew. Thank you, Claire.

Foreword

You may think not another management book! But this one is by an author who has been there and produced results for small businesses who strive to be bigger.

This book is about self-awareness and what you need to know about yourself and others to really make a difference to a small business and how to make it thrive.

Lots of parables and sound advice to achieve the "big dream" with advice on how to overcome setbacks along the way to sustained success.

Well worth a read.

Sir Peter Bonfield CBE FREng

Sir Peter Bonfield is a leading International Business Executive with over forty five years' experience in the fields of electronics, computers and communications. Since 2002 Sir Peter has been involved with a diverse portfolio of companies operating at main Board level in the USA, Europe and the Far East. Change management in international technology companies has characterised his work.

This is a book of generous spirit; it is like having your own personal coach and though you may not have met Phil, his voice and his experience ring out of the pages loud and clear. The size of your company should not be a limit to your dreams or your ambition. We have a saying in Zen "if only death is certain but the manner and time of your death is uncertain, what should you do now?" Take the opportunities you have and that this book encourages you to take.

Claire Genkai Breeze
Partner, Relume Ltd, co-founder, the other 980, and co-author 'The Challenger Spirit'

It is no surprise that Phil has felt compelled to share his perspectives on transformation with a broader audience. Having experienced, lived through and managed change in a variety of circumstances in a wide variety of national and cultural mix, Phil is well placed to share his insights. I have known Phil since the early 1990's and he has always striven to enable colleagues and clients to benefit from what he has learnt and it is a logical extension that he know chooses to broaden his appeal through this book. I wish him and you every success.

Mike Campbell
Group Director, Transformation, easyJet plc

Like many businesses, mine was born from personal dreams and ambitions.

Philip's book aims to make dreams become reality, enabling one's business to become the best it wants to be. It is an excellent guide for the small business seeking to develop and improve.

It is ideally designed for the busy individual to be able to dip in and out for the advice relevant to specific challenges and opportunities. I especially liked the bonus materials providing exercises to assist in transforming your business. It is obvious that Philip has a vast range of experience in business transformation and development, and the book enables the reader to make the most of those years of experience.

I can't wait to see what a difference I can make to my business using the techniques, and have no hesitation in recommending the book to other business owners – or people who dream of owning a profitable business of their own!!

Jackie Chappell
Owner, The Ironing Lady Ltd and The Cleaning Ladies Ltd
and former Chief Executive, Rail Industry Training Council

This book provides wise counsel to small businesses about how they can be creative, engaging and innovative in transforming their business. Too many business/management authors concentrate on the corporates, this book is a useful addition to the literature to help develop the SME sector in the UK and beyond.

Professor Cary L Cooper CBE
Distinguished Professor of Organizational Psychology and Health, Lancaster University Management School

I would like to say I enjoyed the book immensely. It is easy to read, easy to understand and any chapter at any time has relevance. I would urge anyone to read it, digest it and take action. Years of experience in a book full of golden nuggets.

Richard Knight
Owner, Focal Point Advertising Ltd and Chair of FSB East Berkshire branch

Philip's book gives interesting insight into the challenge of managing change and he deals with the road blocks that so often bedevil transformation. If you want to raise your business to another level this is a book that you should read.

David Knowles-Leak
Founder dkl Accelerating Performance, FSB Director and Thames Valley Regional Chairman

Whether as individuals or small enterprises, we all experience barriers to realising our potential. This book uses the powerful imagery of the title to help us overcome those barriers with reflective tools, relevant examples and lively practical advice. One to keep handy, dip into from time to time, and share and discuss with the team. It is certain to take you forward on your business journey.

Andrew Mayo
Professor of Human Capital Management, Middlesex University and Director, Mayo Learning International Ltd

The lessons of the book about both business and personal transformation have great resonance, some almost throwaway lines having significant value, hence encouraging re-reading of this modestly sized book to pick up the valuable thoughts that may elude a first read... The attraction of the book is particularly in its identification of core issues in managing transformations, particularly against opposition, such as communications planning, project managing, handling setbacks, engagement of stakeholders, and advocating change. Thus any person involved in contributing to a change programme in any scale of business can benefit from the ideas the author shares on these issues... All the author has to say about carrying out changes in a business will resonate with readers who have been in such a process as instigators, advisers or even perhaps victims of a change process.

Michael Sippitt
Chairman, Clarkslegal LLP

There are thousands of books encouraging us to learn what to do to succeed in business but very few that give us the secrets of HOW to do it. In Dance with the Elephants Philip gives some of the simple yet powerful secrets to success and does so generously and efficiently. I have in practice danced with elephants in India and it is a life changing experience. This book could not be more aptly titled.

Sue Knight, NLP Master Trainer and author of 'NLP at Work'

Contents

Why Transform?

Is it for you?

Would you like to get to the end of your life feeling that you have achieved everything you could possibly dream of for you and your small business?

Would you like to know that people will celebrate your life because you left a momentous legacy for others and lasting memories of all you achieved?

Would you like to bask in the glory of having lived your life to the full – knowing that you and your business had been the best you wanted to be, for you and for others?

What is business transformation? Can you do it?

Transformation is about far more than change. Think about what happens when you freeze water. From ice, you can create something entirely new such as a beautiful ice sculpture. While it is still fundamentally water, it is now completely different in form, function and purpose. *That* is a transformation. Remember, if you don't maintain the conditions necessary for the transformation into a beautiful object, it goes back to being just water.

Business transformation works in a similar way. But there is no 'magic wand'. Your business transformation will take a great deal of hard work and determination, and you are likely to feel uncomfortable at times.

So, before you read further, ask yourself first whether you are:

- Committed to transforming your established business into a super-successful business?

- Determined to take things to the next level and really grow your efficiency, revenues and profits?

- Prepared to examine whether the firm grip you have on your business is perhaps constraining it?

If you answered 'yes', read on, this book is for you.

You're committed; what next?

Transformation works for all shapes and sizes of business. Whether your business consists of just you, or whether you employ others, the tools and techniques outlined here will work equally well.

Even if you are a sole trader with no employees, you don't exist in isolation. You have many stakeholders such as customers, suppliers, partners and those you would like to be customers. In your personal life you have friends, family and acquaintances. You may be a member of a business organisation, a club or a gym. Everyone you meet can be resources to call on to help you with your business transformation.

If you do employ people in your business, they are additional stakeholders who can help with your business transformation. This book enables you to effectively engage all your stakeholders to support you in achieving your transformation, whatever their relationship with you.

Here's a great way to get started. Tell all your stakeholders that you are reading this book and, most importantly, tell them why. Tell them what you want your business to achieve. If you actually had that magic wand, what would you wish for? The more people you tell, the more comfortable you will become with your vision, and the greater your commitment will be to your business transformation.

Why I wrote this book

I decided to write this book to reach many more people like you. My whole philosophy, my raison d'être, my purpose in life is to give people the choice of being the best they want to be, not just the best they can be.

My commitment to my clients is to help them decide how good they want to be, to enable them to achieve that, and also to transfer new skills to them and their businesses to make them self-sufficient in being the best they want to be. This book was written to help you acquire the necessary mindset, tools and techniques.

I have been accountable for business transformations for many years, undertaking my first assignment at a very tender age. That transformation turned a field of sheep into a leading manufacturing facility. My speciality and my passion have always been to take an existing business and transform it through step changes in performance.

I wrote this book so you can achieve transformational results like those that have been achieved by organisations I have worked with in the past; for example:

- quadrupled revenues in less than four years

- increased profitability by 23% in just one year

- taken £8 million of cost out of a business in six months

- broken into the top ten suppliers in their chosen market in three years, from a position outside the top 100

- delivered industry-leading levels of customer satisfaction with over 60% saying 'very satisfied' and 'extremely satisfied', and only 2.3% dissatisfied in an industry with dissatisfaction levels around 50%.

How to approach this book

How you read this book is up to you. If you wish, start at page 1 and read on to the end. However, I didn't write this book by starting at the beginning. Instead, I took the topic about which I was most passionate, that was most relevant at the time, and then sat down to write. So, if you wish, feel free to dip in and out of the book, focusing on whatever grabs your attention. This has the added advantage of allowing you to align your reading to your interest and passion at the time.

Whichever way you choose to read it, this book can be read in about two hours. I know what it's like to run a small business and how little free time there is, so I do appreciate the commitment required.

At the end of each chapter, you will find a handy section called 'The essence of this chapter' which summarises the most important points.

At the back of the book, you will find a list of bonus materials that are available free from the official website of this book (www.dancewiththeelephants.com) and a chart linking each to the relevant chapter. You will find it useful to have these bonus materials to hand when reading the chapter.

The bonus materials will be expanded over time, and I hope that people will help me with this enlargement. There is a community of Dancers with Elephants to share with and learn from that you can access at the website, and it is through this community that I hope we can develop additional material.

I wish you every success as your small business learns to thrive, to grow and to reward you with everything you ever dreamed of at the outset. I hope this book and the bonus materials will help you to successfully 'Dance with the Elephants' that represent the bigger businesses you want to compete successfully with in the future. Read more about Elephants next!

Good luck and great Dancing!

Philip I Walker

Elephants!

This book is called 'Dance with the Elephants' for three reasons. First, as a small business, you really can Dance with big business Elephants. Lou Gerstner, who ran IBM, entitled his book 'Who Says Elephants Can't Dance?' Of course big businesses can Dance, and his transformation of IBM went a long way to prove that. But, when they Dance, they still Dance like Elephants. As the 'Age of the Entrepreneur' evolves, big businesses are increasingly worried about competition from small businesses. This book will enable you to transform your small business not only to Dance with the Elephants but to prove that, when small businesses Dance, they are far more nimble and elegant than the big business Elephants.

The second reason for the title is because the production of it has been a Dance with an Elephant for me. I wrote this, my first book, in collaboration with (and I'm sure he'll take this in the way it is intended) an Elephant in the world of authors, Raymond Aaron, who has been my guide and mentor. Raymond is co-author of the New York Times best-seller 'Chicken Soup for the Parent's Soul' and author of the Canadian best-seller 'Chicken Soup for the Canadian Soul'. He has written several other successful books, and he Dances rather well. I am certainly not an Elephant in his world, but he has kindly agreed to Dance with me to get this book into your hands.

Thirdly, when we think about Elephants, often what we think about is 'The Elephant in the Room' – the Elephant that nobody will attend to. So often these Elephants are the reason we can't move forward; they prevent us from transforming our businesses because we choose not to address them. Ironically, the Elephant in the Room is frequently why we don't Dance with the Elephants. I want you to be able to take on your Elephants so you can succeed in transforming your small business. This book and the bonus materials are designed to support you in this.

The Elephants in our lives

Let's look at the Elephants that exist in our lives and in our businesses. Maybe you'll recognise some of these colourful Elephants.

The Blue Elephant represents the people around us who are mostly down or depressed or blue. They hold us back because they are just so depressing. How can you Dance when you are depressed? These Elephants are too depressed to Dance, and their depressive gloom can prevent us from Dancing too.

The Red Elephant is a symbol of the people around us who are angry most of the time. The reason why they're angry isn't important – they just are. They are too angry to Dance and so stop us Dancing too. If their anger includes being angry with you, Dancing with you is naturally out of the question!

The Yellow Elephant denotes the people around us who are cowardly, timid or fearful. Their fear overwhelms them. They are too afraid to Dance, restricted by concerns such as health & safety. They say 'Dancing with Elephants is just too risky, so nobody should do it'.

Then we have the Black Elephant symbolising the people around us who are nihilistic. 'It's not possible to Dance with the Elephants and there's no point even if it were possible.' They blow out any flickering flame of hope. Their world is black and dark, and doesn't involve Dance.

What about the Magnolia Elephant? Have you ever noticed when you go into a new property that the prevailing colour is magnolia? Magnolia is designed not to offend, to be bland, to be inconspicuous. There may be a Dance but it's so subtle, so unremarkable, that it is hardly noticeable. The Elephants that Dance are remarkable, not magnolia.

Then we find the envious Green Elephant. Green Elephants spend all their energy on the achievements of others, wondering why others have more than they have. They desire to be better, but focus only on why their lot in life is so inferior to that of other people instead of getting on with transforming their own lot. They watch others Dance, and rage inside at the injustice.

Next is the Sepia Elephant, obsessed with the 'Golden Age' when things were so perfect – an Age that can never be recreated. In their heart of hearts, no matter what they do now or in the future, nothing can be as good as back then. They long for the Dance that once was, not the Dances that could be.

You may find the Plaid Elephant, the multi-coloured Elephant. These people try to be all things to all people at all times. When you ask 'Who is our best customer, our target customer?' they may be the people in your small business who respond 'Everybody!' Hopelessly lacking focus, they want to Dance with everybody rather than taking action to find the best Elephants to Dance with.

Next you might recognise the Steel Elephant which symbolises the people who are all about hard, cold facts. They have little interest in imagination, emotion or passion. 'Show me the facts now, rather than imagining what it would be like to Dance with the Elephants!'

Or you may have encountered the Sky-Blue Pink Elephants. These people are 'away with the fairies'. They love to dream, they dream to live, but they do very little. They are good at dreaming about how it would be to Dance with the Elephants, but you will never see them on the Dance floor.

Or what about the Yellow Polka Dot Elephant? Yellow Polka Dot as in the old song 'Itsy Bitsy Teenie Weenie Yellow Polka Dot Bikini'. These are the dedicated followers of fashion! They relentlessly pursue the latest fashion, whether or not it's relevant to the business. Find these Elephants by listening for their language. They talk endlessly about implementing best practice within your business, spending their time looking at what other people are doing to implement the latest best practices. Instead of creating differentiation for your small business, they're trying to make it look like everybody else's. Don't get me wrong, there are some benefits from implementing best practice. I'm a fan of whatever works well. But slavishly implementing what the Elephants have already done doesn't necessarily enable you to Dance with the Elephants successfully.

What about the Grey Elephant? This Elephant represents the dull, the boring, the mind-numbing. The Grey Elephant doesn't Dance. Dancing is too exciting. They prefer their familiar and comfortable ennui.

How many of the coloured Elephants have you recognised that may now be in the Rooms of your small business? Perhaps they have been in the Room with you in the past, and you decided not to address them. This book, along with the bonus materials available from the official website of the book will help you to address the Elephants in your Rooms. I will show you how to get even these Elephants to Dance.

I will also show you how to Dance with the Elephants that represent far bigger companies that are Dancing in your marketplaces. My intention is not to turn you into an Elephant but to help you Dance with them!

The essence of this chapter: Small businesses can Dance with much larger businesses (Elephants). The Elephants in the Room of our small businesses can prevent you from Dancing with the Elephants in your marketplaces. Bonus materials are available from the book's website. This book will enable you to transform your small business into big profits.

8

Your notes

If you wish, use this page to record the actions you will take.

Big Dreams, Crafted Well, Engaging All

A big bold dream, beautifully described, is immensely powerful. This chapter will help you dream your Big Dream, and describe it beautifully, in a way that truly engages your spirit and resources. It will enable you to engage those around you to help you achieve your successful transformation. Before we explore further, I want to reflect on how people interact with their worlds in different ways. We will get to your Big Dream, but understanding how people interact with their worlds is a useful starting point because it will enable you to engage the widest range of stakeholders who may support you.

Have you ever noticed the people who are always talking about the past, bringing most conversations around to how things used to be? On the other hand, what about people who are so focused on the possibilities of the future that they devote their energies to what could be, instead of what used to be? Or, how about those who live for the moment, seeming only to care about now! These three groups experience the world using different windows, or filters. When they meet, they may find they are at cross purposes and their language is noticeably different. People who use the same filters tend to connect better with each other.

How people experience the world

The ability to recognise and use different filters is a 'learnable skill'. We use many different filters, for example we often use time filters when interacting with our worlds. For now, let's think about the three filters of time – the past, present and future – as described in the scenario above.

In an organisation, it is really helpful to have a balanced mixture of all the time filters. I recall working with one established team with a very strong tendency to focus on their future plans, on what it would mean for them to realise their goals. They spent little time thinking about what they had done in the past, about what had worked or not been so successful for them and so they were unlikely to learn from the past. As the quote from George Santanya goes: 'Those who cannot remember the past are condemned to repeat it.'

So focused was this team on their future plans that they found it really difficult to focus on the first steps that they could take in the here and now to achieve their grand ambitions. They were known by other teams in the same organisation as the 'dream weavers' and were not viewed as particularly helpful or popular.

I had been asked to work with them to see if I could help them change their behaviours, to learn the lessons of the past and look at the practicalities of the here and now, so that they could implement things effectively. It took a little time. Behaviour change is not quick and easy as anyone who has given up smoking or lost weight will tell you. But the team got there in the end, becoming more balanced across the three perspectives of time.

When taking on the assignment, I asked whether the organisation could utilise the 'dream weavers' in an effective way. Who did the dreaming for the organisation? Unsurprisingly, the responsibility for dreaming about the future lay with the business owner. This may be true in your own organisation. The business owner later formed an informal group with several of the dream weavers to think of different possibilities for the organisation, meeting quarterly.

Using all five senses

People use many other filters. Some process their interactions with the world largely in terms of their visual systems. These people will ask questions such as 'Do you see what I mean?' or respond 'I can see that' or 'The way I look at it is …'. Mostly they use visual language and visual metaphors.

Other people tend to 'hear' their worlds. They say things like 'I heard that', 'I hear what you are saying' or 'It sounds like …'. Their primary way of interfacing with the world is auditory.

A third group experience their worlds more in terms of feelings, and so tend to speak about emotions and use emotional language as they interact with the world. You may hear them say things like 'I feel excited about that', 'I feel I understand how important this is to you' or 'I'm feeling unsure about that'. Their primary interaction with the world is expressed in emotions and feelings.

Less frequently seen than the visual, auditory and feelings filters, are two other groups which process their interactions with the world more in terms of what they taste and what they smell. As they recall a pleasurable experience in the past, they may talk about the smell they can recall or the taste of the experience.

Having learned about the different ways that people interact with their worlds, we can now move on to your Big Dream.

Dreaming big

Big Dreams are much more powerful when they are communicated using as many of the different filters as possible, in order to connect with the widest range of people. One of the challenges of Dancing with the Elephants is to give ourselves permission to dream big and to dream well. Dreaming big is important since Big Dreams lead to stretching goals that are the very essence of transformational change as opposed to incremental change. Asking and answering the question 'What do I really want?' involves giving ourselves permission to dream big. It's very easy to limit our dreams to what we think is reasonable and achievable. But, if we are able to dream big, to really fire our imaginations about how we would like the world to be for us, we can give ourselves permission to dream the unlikely, and even the unthinkable.

The very act of dreaming the unthinkable, of letting fantasy shape our dreams more than reality, gives us access to the art of the possible instead of the art of the likely. To be truly the best we want to be, we have to remove the inhibitions and the limiting assumptions that have been poured into us from an early age. So often our processing is at the level of the 'other-than-conscious mind'; we almost run on autopilot. We unconsciously delete many possibilities for our futures without realising what is going on in the other-than-conscious mind: for example, perhaps our upbringing taught us that modesty is worthy. If we apply this filter and moderate our Big Dreams, we risk losing possibilities. We may not even be aware of their loss.

Giving yourself permission to dream big is the first step on the road to transformation. It is not only about what you really want, about dreaming without bounds, it is also about the quality of the dreaming, both for ourselves and for other people. This is another learnable skill.

If we give ourselves permission to dream, we can more easily process and communicate our dreams using all of our five senses (sight, hearing, feelings, smell and taste). The more we can use the five senses, the more we are able to engage a wide assortment of people who will be able to connect with our dreams and give us vital support for our transformational changes and goals. By communicating through all the senses, you greatly increase the number of people who can relate to your dreams because we tend to connect with other people's dreams more quickly and naturally when their messages are expressed using our primary way of interacting with the world. I hope you have come to understand how dreaming big, and expressing those dreams well, will help you to engage a wide range of people to support you in your transformational journey.

As well as engaging them, there is another reason to express your dream to others. Expressing your dream in the form of commitments you make to yourself, in the presence of others, strengthens your sense of commitment. It also increases the likelihood that you will be successful. There is little as powerful as expressing out loud, in front of others, a commitment you intend to keep.

Making the Big Dream real

As well as engaging others, expressing your Big Dream, or Big Dreams, to yourself is important. The very act of expressing your dreams across each of the five senses will make your dreams seem far more real to you. The whole process of articulating your dreams through the five senses enables your conscious and other-than-conscious minds to connect better and more fully with your dreams. The more you are able to 'live' your dream in your mind before you even start on your journey of transformation, the more real that dream will become to you.

Remember, the more you focus on the future you want to create, the less space there is within you for that which you have to let go. The quicker you let go of the old, the sooner you find the new.

Certain things are important to link you to the future you want to create and to make your dream seem more real, more desirable and more achievable. One of these is self-talking about your dream, hearing how the world will be when your dream is achieved, visualising your dream in your mind's eye. Also, imagining how you will feel, tasting the fruits of success, and smelling what will be around you in your transformed world. Ultimately, to 'live' your dream in your imagination through all your senses prepares you to be the best you want to be.

As you dream your Big Dream, how will you know when you've achieved your dream? Ask yourself what evidence you would need to prove that your dream really has been achieved. These questions will help you identify the evidence across all five senses:

What will you be seeing when you've got it?
What will you be hearing when you've got it?
What will you be feeling when you've got it?
What will you taste when you've got it?
What will you smell when you've got it?
What will others see you doing when you've got it?
What will others hear you saying when you've got it?
How will others feel when your dream has become reality?

When you dream, it's important that the output is expressed positively – that is, a positive expression of what you want rather than a negative expression of what you don't want. After all, we tend to get what we focus on. Tell a child not to fall off, and they automatically think about falling off. Tell them to stay on, and their mind is set on staying on. That's how our brains work: if I tell you not to think about a Blue Elephant, your brain first has to think about a Blue Elephant and then must try to remove the thought.

Small dreams lead to Big Dreams

Often when we dare to dream big, it is an incremental process. The way to build the small dreams at each step into bigger dreams is to ask yourself the question 'If I had that, what would that do for me?' at each step. Or 'If I had that, what would then become possible?' As the dream gets bigger and bigger, you may want to remember how the journey first started. As well as being able to describe your Big Dream in all five senses to both yourself and to others, you can also relate how your Big Dream evolved, telling the story to increase engagement. We all love stories and are highly engaged when they are told well.

Building the dream

As you finally reach understanding of your Big Dream, a reality check is most useful. This is the point at which you have to ask yourself whether you are able to start and then to maintain the actions necessary to get the results you are

16

looking for. It may be that you need some additional resources to enable you to either start or maintain the journey. The Big Dream is yours: it needs to be something that you can start and maintain with the resources available to you. It cannot be dependent on somebody else either starting or maintaining it. While you may have help in developing and expressing your Big Dream, the ultimate responsibility has to be yours.

There are three additional stages to build your Big Dream.

First you must think about when, where and with whom you want your dream to become reality. It's worthwhile considering how long you want it for. Is this to become a permanent state or a short-lived transition towards an even better state?

The next stage is about positive by-products, and to illustrate this I'd like to share a story from my past. I was working with a client who was desperate to give up smoking. She had tried many different options in her eight-year quest to kick the habit. She did give up smoking, and the method that worked for her was perhaps a little surprising. I asked her to think about the positive by-products of *not* giving up smoking – that is, the good things that not giving up gave her. She initially thought this a little counter-intuitive and wanted to focus on how to give up but, perhaps exasperated that nothing else had worked so far, she agreed to work with me on identifying these positive by-products. We found several. Smoking with work colleagues was social, it gave her a sense of relaxation and, most tellingly of all, she realised it gave her informal and regular access to the MD of the company who was also a smoker. She came to understand that this was perhaps a crucial positive by-product. It gave her a close relationship with somebody very influential in her career, provided her with the opportunity to learn different aspects of the business that she might otherwise not have been privy to, and offered her a better understanding of some senior-level politics. Together we developed an action plan to give my client regular access to the MD without cigarettes being involved. She put together ways in which she could still get informal and quality time with the MD, ways that did not involve standing outside the building in all weathers smoking. She also engaged the MD in her enterprise, explaining what she was hoping to achieve and what assistance he could give her. Within three months she had given up smoking. Her plans were successful because we went through each of the positive by-products and found ways of giving her access to each in a way that did not involve smoking. To summarise this second stage, the question to ask yourself is 'What do I get out of my present situation that I want to keep?'

The last stage is to ask yourself whether the benefits you will get from realising your dream will be worth the cost to you. There is always a cost to you. Obviously, the bigger the benefit of your transformational change to you, the higher the cost you will be able to bear. Remember that the cost is not merely financial; you also have to ask if it is worth the time it's going to take you.

Time for that honesty check

Finally, ask yourself the question of congruence. In fact, congruence is a theme that will re-occur several times in this book. Ask yourself if the outcome that you desire is truly in keeping with your sense of self. This really is the honesty check question. Is the new world that you will inhabit when you have realised your Big Dream really the world that sits most comfortably with you, with your over-riding sense of purpose? As they say 'Be careful what you wish for!'

You can obtain some powerful bonus materials from the book's website. In conjunction with the chapter of the book entitled *Your Congruence is Vital*, the bonus material *A Model for Alignment* is helpful. The bonus materials *From Cynical to Committed* and *Elegant Communication Framework* are also germane.

The essence of this chapter: To transform your small business into big profits you must dream Big, Well-Crafted Dreams. In doing so you will be able, with the help of this book and the bonus materials, to fully engage and focus you and your internal resources. You will also be able to engage all the stakeholders you will need to support your transformation. Your dreams have to be bold enough to really attract the people that are able to help you. They must also be sufficiently bold to repel those who will not help you. Your Big Dreams will bring those who can help to Dance with the Elephants with you and make it possible for those who cannot help to go Dance somewhere else. Later chapters in the book, and the bonus materials on the website, will help you get more people into the right groups for them, and fewer people sitting watching the Dance Floor from the balcony.

Your notes

If you wish, use this page to record the actions you will take.

Your Congruence is Vital

To Dance successfully with the Elephants in your marketplace, you must Dance your own Dance. Don't Dance their Dance or some other Dance you think will allow you to flourish but does not truly represent who you are and what you stand for. To compete with and win against these Elephants, your customers, prospective clients and all your stakeholders must experience the true essence of you and your company in all their dealings with you. As the best-selling author Simon Sinek explains in his 2009 book 'Start With Why: How Great Leaders Inspire Everyone to Take Action', people do not buy *what* you do, they buy *why* you do it.

You are your business brand

The smaller your business, the more your business brand is *you*. Even when there is just you in your business, it is challenging to keep everything that happens in that business aligned and fully representative of your Big Dream. We humans can quite easily be moved out of congruence with our Big Dream by external events, by factors beyond our control and by the Big Dreams of others. Not only do such external events blow us off course, but we are pretty good at diverging from congruence with our Big Dream and 'Well-Formed Outcomes' through our own efforts, or lack thereof. Well-Formed Outcomes are the expression of your Big Dream in as many of the filters as possible. These efforts are not always the result of conscious decisions, but often occur at the behest of our other-than-conscious mind. The other-than-conscious mind operates our bodies through a series of automatic, pre-programmed responses, formed we know not when, as the results of circumstances we no longer recall. Although we should honour our history and learn from it, we should not allow it to define or confine our future.

As your small business grows, and more people become involved, keeping congruence becomes more about aligning other people, although your personal congruence is still vital. The chapter **Congruent Elephants and Other Creatures** will cover in more detail how you can get other people aligned and congruent with your transformation, with your Well-Formed Outcome, with your Big Dream.

Aligning yourself

Here I want to concentrate on your personal congruence, on your ability to keep in alignment. The bonus material **A Model for Alignment** is available from the website. It will be useful for you to have it available as we explore the model here.

The other useful thing for you to bring to the work in this chapter is your curiosity. I hope you will reflect and will ask yourself some deep and personal questions. Be curious about the questions and curious about your reactions and responses to them. Don't judge any of the questions, your reactions or your responses. Don't label them as 'right' or 'wrong, 'good' or 'bad', 'silly' or 'sound'. Instead explore the 'What if?' approach. By way of practice, take a look at the Model for Alignment and be curious about what would be possible by working with it. Don't label it as either a 'good model' or a 'bad model'. Reflect on your world through the prism of the model and be curious about your reactions as you do so. You will find that the learnable skill to place curiosity over judgement will help you tremendously if you adopt this approach while you are enabling congruence in others.

The Model for Alignment recognises that we interact with our world at different logical levels, ranging from environmental factors, through our behaviours, our capabilities and skills, our beliefs and values and, by way of our very identity, into our overall sense of purpose. The model acknowledges the different natures of these interactions. Your target is to have all logical levels aligned with your Big Dream, your Well-Formed Outcome, your overriding sense of purpose – each of which should be perfectly congruent with each other in order for your transformation to be successful.

Aligning environmental factors. We experience our physical environment in a way that is either congruent or incongruent with who we really are, with our sense of purpose, with our Big Dream. If our environment is not congruent, things seem a little off. For example, if you are a retailer who wants to delight customers with your calm, professional and attentive service ethos, it probably would be incongruous to have heavy rock music pounding out in your store. The secret is to get the environment into congruence with all the higher level factors.

Aligning behaviour. Let's continue with our retail example. At the next level up, it would be incongruent behaviour for the staff to be anything but calm, professional and attentive. Behaviour such as not making eye contact or chatting with colleagues instead of focusing on customers would be inconsistent with alignment, projecting the wrong messages to both customers and prospective customers. So it's important to make sure that our behaviours are aligned: 'Is what I am actually doing true to who I really am?'

Aligning capabilities and skills. How we use our capabilities and skills should also be congruent. This is about maximising our potential, using all of our skills and knowledge, and doing so in the best possible way. If you don't have the necessary skills needed to support your Big Dream, this will become evident at some point to your customers and to those you would like to be your customers. The old adage of 'Do only what you are good at' is particularly apt. It has long been my view that we should do more and more of what we are good at, what we enjoy and what represents our natural talents, and do less and less of what we find to be the opposite. The more you focus on capabilities and skills that suit you, the more aligned you are with your beliefs and values, your identity and your overall sense of purpose.

Aligning values and beliefs. Just as your capabilities and skills need to be in alignment, all interactions you have with stakeholders should be congruent with your values and beliefs. You should focus on living your values and beliefs in all your interactions. The exercise which is available as a bonus material from the website, *Your Purpose in Life: The Values You Hold Dear*, will help you to define your values and to identify your real purpose in life. The more you can be congruent with your true values and beliefs, the more people will recognise who you are, what you believe in and what you value. If they are clear about your beliefs and values, and you live your life in ways that are consistent with them, people will see that you are genuine and align more comfortably with you.

Aligning our identity. At the top of the hierarchy of interactions with our worlds is our identity, who we really are. We are complex creatures and we all have a self-image. Some people have a very clear understanding of who they are, and they have this understanding consistently. At times, some people lose their clarity about who they are, they may lose confidence, and they may find life quite hard because they are not clear about who they are. The work I do with clients reconnects them with, or redefines, who they are. Identity, positioned as it is at the top of the hierarchy, is very important to achieving your transformation as it is the beacon that attracts stakeholders who can support your transformation.

Am I who I want to be?

People want to be true to who they are, but sometimes find it a struggle. I recall working with one woman who wanted to redefine her relationship with a long-term friend, with whom she had previously been very close, intimate even. She felt the relationship had taken too much out of her emotionally, and so wanted to move on and have less interaction with her old friend. However, she saw herself as a compassionate person who was sufficiently skilled to not cause anyone to feel hurt by her actions. In this instance, her identity meant she could not hurt her old friend by changing the relationship in the way that she wanted. So important was her identity as a caring person who would not hurt her friend that she didn't feel able to have an adult conversation with her friend about why she wanted to change the relationship. Instead she chose to continue with the pain of the relationship, choosing a strategy of very gradual withdrawal over a year or 18 months to establish the new relationship. She chose to experience pain over an extended period rather than putting into question her self-image of never hurting anyone in any way.

Actually, we can choose our identity – even in the face of all the labels, stereotypes and straitjackets that are attributed to us by other people. We can choose not to be defined by others. Just as importantly, we can choose consciously to define our identity rather than letting it be defined by our past experiences and their impact on our other-than-conscious minds. Work through the exercises in the *Your Purpose in Life: The Values You Hold Dear* bonus material to help you gain clarity on your purpose in life and greater understanding of your values.

When you are aligned at all logical levels, people will be certain about you. Some people will decide not to align with you. This is good because it is a genuine choice based on understanding and incompatibility. You don't want to waste your energies trying to align with these people. Those who really get you will choose to align with you.

I want to commend to you the work of Daniel H. Pink on the subject. His book, 'Drive: The Surprising Truth About What Motivates Us', and an excellent animated video of him speaking on the RSA website are worth checking out (www.thersa.org).

Have no fear

Make sure that all activities at every logical level are aligned and congruent with your overriding sense of purpose and with all the other levels. Where there is incongruence at any level, take action and be bold. As you seek to make the incongruence congruent, ask yourself what you would do if you had no fear?

If your environment really should be in the heart of a bustling conurbation and you are actually in the middle of nowhere, what would you do if you had no fear?

If you really should speak Mandarin to communicate with your current and emerging suppliers, but you only speak your mother tongue, what would you do if you had no fear?

If your target market is filled with dedicated parachutists who prefer to buy from people like them, but you have never jumped out of an airplane, what would you do if you had no fear?

Five additional tools

Ambition

I want to stress the importance of ambition as the first tool you can use to develop and sustain your congruence in addition to the Model for Alignment. It is important to develop ambition as part of your congruence as it will attract people who identify with your challenges, your standards and the striving nature that underlies your ambition. They will be attracted by your courage, your boldness and your integrity. Cultivate ambition beyond the current resources of your business and your stakeholders, and beyond your current personal resources. Such stretching ambition will proclaim that you are, or will be, the best at something. Something you want to make a stand for. Something your customers, prospective customers and people can fall in love with. Something they can hold you accountable for.

Hope

Build hope into your congruence. What is it you hope for? How can you express what you hope for in visual, verbal and sensory language? Hope is another element that your stakeholders will need from you to enable them to be congruent with you and your transformation. What hoped-for things will people see, hear and feel?

Brand

Create passionate personal meaning within you about your transformation, and rehearse the different ways in which you will communicate your passion. Think of your passionate commitment as a deep *covenant*. Build a brand that expresses what you stand for, what you believe in, why you do what you do. Since the brand of a business is the third biggest driver of employee engagement globally, build a strong brand that your employees can relate to and eulogise about. Many case studies show that improved employee engagement flows straight to the bottom line; organisations with high levels of employee engagement deliver higher shareholder returns, greater sales per employee and stronger levels of customer loyalty than those with medium or low levels of engagement. Engaged organisations also have lower levels of absence and greater employee loyalty as evidenced by staff retention levels, plus they are more innovative. Building a strong brand that employees rave about delivers top- and bottom-line results.

I want you to focus on how you can create and sustain a brand that represents your cause, your calling, your passion. It should faithfully embody that which you would die for. You want employees to love your brand. You want customers to love your brand. You certainly want prospective customers to love your brand. What do you truly love? What are you sincerely smitten by? What can you passionately commit to?

Trust

As you build your brand, make sure that you build in trust. How will you ensure that the promises inherent in your brand will always be delivered? 'A brand is a promise kept.' If you can't trust your brand, others will struggle to do so. Your employees need to completely get why you do what you do, what your overriding purpose is, and what values your business stands for. Your brand should be trusted at every one of the logical levels identified in the Model for Alignment. Your entire business and every single transaction should be designed around delivering your trusted brand. All of which means you have to be entirely congruent with regards to your trusted brand.

We have come to understand that your personal congruence is vital to your successful transformation. I cover getting congruence in others in another chapter, and will include how to address the Elephants (and other creatures) in the Rooms of your small business.

Focus

I want to draw your attention to one final element of your personal congruence. That is, the more focused and narrowly-defined your congruence is, the more successful you will be in attracting fans.

Business transformations fail where they attempt to be all things to all people. They fail where target customers are defined as 'Everybody!' (Remember the Plaid Elephant?) They fail where the products or services are defined as, or pretty close to, 'Everything!' They fail where their niche is ill-defined, and insufficiently focused on the very specific needs of a clearly delineated set of potential customers.

Elephant companies in your marketplace do not personalise their offerings as well as smaller, more nimble and more dynamic competitors such as your small business. Operating in a clearly defined niche allows you to personalise your offerings to the very specific needs of your target customers. Don't misinterpret me by assuming you can only operate in one very small niche to be successful. You can operate in more than one niche as long as it's clear to your target customers in that niche that you are totally focused on their specific and distinct needs and desires. In each niche, deploy marketing with a strength of message that is strong enough to attract your ideal customers, and sufficiently robust to repel those time-wasters who would distract you and dissipate your resources.

Living in Two Worlds

Having now covered all the elements of your personal congruence, I feel it only fair to address the 'Two Worlds' challenge that you will face as the leader of your transformation. You will be living concurrently in two very different worlds as you travel on your journey of transformation, and it can even seem somewhat schizophrenic at times. The best way to explain this is by sharing a specific episode from my own Two Worlds experience.

I was asked to join an organisation to design and deliver a five-year transformational plan. I'll call this World Two because it was the world of transformation. It was focused on the goals for each of the five years, where each year's revenue target was based on the end point five years ahead. The targets were not based on increments derived from past performance. Unfortunately (but for very good reasons), the five-year plan was known only to a few people. This meant that almost everybody else lived in World One. In World One, revenue targets were monthly and only went as far as the end of the current fiscal year. Hence, in April at the start of the year, there were 12 targets to hit. In July, there were nine targets left to hit, and so on. Everything was focused on the current month and the current year, with no thought about future years for the inhabitants of World One. Revenue targets were based on what happened in the same period last year, adding an increment to keep everybody busy.

I also lived in World One. My performance, and compensation, was driven by achieving the monthly, quarterly and annual revenue targets. The problem of living in Two Worlds was illustrated at the end of the first year. World One had met all the targets and everyone was pleased. Then the World One revenue targets for year two were published by the finance team, who were blissfully unaware of World Two and the five-year plan. The full-year revenue target for World One they set was about 15% lower than the target World Two needed to meet the five-year plan. All of a sudden, living in Two Worlds was an uncomfortable place for me. Together with all the other World One citizens, I could succeed in World One and create an even larger future mountain to climb in World Two – and only a very few people would know we were storing up a future problem. Fortunately, I managed to persuade the sales teams to set and achieve year two targets 20% above those set by the finance team. Persuading them was not easy, but their over-achievement against the original finance targets (the basis of the sales compensation plan) meant they were all very handsomely rewarded that year. We went on to achieve our five-year World Two target in year four.

Living in Two Worlds won't always have such good results for you – but good results are still possible. Becoming comfortable with grappling with your Two Worlds will contribute to the success of your transformation. You have to deliver the business-as-usual performance that is based on historical achievements, and help your stakeholders to do so too. You also have to get personally comfortable with addressing the much more stretching challenges of World Two that are the consequences of your transformational commitments. Your people also have to be able to deliver World Two performances and your role is to enable them to do just that without dropping the ball in World One.

The essence of this chapter: Live your transformation in all you do. Keeping yourself congruent with your Big Dream(s) in everything you do is vital to the success of your transformation. When you are fully congruent at all logical levels, you enable customers and potential customers to fully understand your purpose in life and to engage with that purpose, with your business and with you individually. People buy *why* you do, not *what* you do. They buy the authenticity and passion of other people. Focus on a niche market, or on a small number of niche markets. Be bold when ensuring you are fully aligned and congruent at all logical levels – what would you do if you had no fear? Push your ambitions beyond the current resources of your business, your stakeholders and you personally. Make sure you do the work that will prepare you to enable congruence in your stakeholders. Ensure your congruence provides them with a sufficiently deep covenant that incorporates the ambition, hope, brand, trust and focus that will create and sustain their versions of personal congruence that will in turn support, nurture and promote yours.

Your notes

If you wish, use this page to record the actions you will take.

Get Creative!

The importance of your transformation programme being based on a Big Dream is outlined in the chapter *Big Dreams, Crafted Well, Engaging All*. For some people, dreaming big comes naturally. For others, this can represent something of a challenge. While my career has involved me in designing and delivering many innovative solutions, my inner voice has always told me that being innovative and creative does not necessarily come naturally to me. Perhaps this is connected to my relative lack of artistic talent, best illustrated by being told 'Don't give up the day job!' during a group exercise that involved me illustrating my thoughts through drawing pictures. It seems I regard creativity and artistic talent as related.

Whether or not my concern about my innate creativity is valid, my response may be seen as a little counter-intuitive. The response was, and continues to be, to use a process called CREATE to achieve creativity.

Open and closed modes

Before I explain this process, let's consider the modes we adopt in our work and in our lives that are relevant to creativity. We humans operate in two different modes. The first is the closed mode, which is the one we operate in most of the time at work. In this mode we are very purposeful, with a sense that there is much to be done, and that we need to get on with it. It is a very active, perhaps even anxious, mode. In this mode creativity is very difficult, if not impossible to access. We get lots done, we are very decisive, and action is the focus of our being. Quite often it is seen as a very efficient way of operating – one that is decisive and gets things done.

Contrast this with the open mode. This is the creative mode. It is often seen as the antithesis of efficiency, the enemy of progress and the domain of the feckless. It may be portrayed as 'lying around', 'shooting the breeze' or 'daydreaming'. While this open, creative mode may be seen in this way by the action junkies who thrive in the closed mode, it is the open mode that is necessary for creativity to exist, flourish and enhance your Big Dreams.

CREATE

The CREATE process has been developed to optimise the creativity of both individuals and teams. I use it when I am working alone and want to maximise my creative capacity. I also use it when working with teams of people or with individual clients. Let me explain the acronym:

C	Cosmos
R	Roster
E	Enhance
A	Assurance
T	The Funny Side
E	Emancipated

C is for Cosmos. The choice of word is deliberate in that it represents moving to a 'different world' – a world that is away from the hurly-burly of the day-to-day operations of the business. It is important to create the right environment for creativity and innovation to emerge. Getting the right physical space, lack of distractions and staying in the open mode is what Cosmos is all about. When I want to be creative, I change my Cosmos. The phone gets switched off, the email is closed down, and any physical manifestations of my day-to-day operations are removed from my sight. It may be that I leave my office to go for a walk, taking my voice recorder with me. I might choose to go to the public library. I might move to a different room and put on some very familiar music that soothes me but does not require my attention. If I am working with others, perhaps with clients, we may leave our normal business environment and spend time in a meeting room, a hotel room or outside at picnic tables. Moving to a different Cosmos tells you, both consciously and at the level of the other-than-conscious mind, that this is going to be different to what you were just doing.

R is for Roster. It is the process of carving time out of the diary in order to enter the open mode and be creative. It is important to ensure that not only is the time allocated within your schedule, but that you also respect the time allocated. There is no point in scheduling, say, 90 minutes for creativity, if during that period you keep returning to closed mode and making decisions about things that have popped into your mind. That these things will pop into your mind is certain. Success comes through having the discipline to focus on the open mode, and honouring time you have allocated to it. This is a learnable skill. The more you can recognise the random thoughts that try to draw you back into the closed mode, and the more you can resist the temptation, the better you will become at this skill.

When I first started to use CREATE I kept post-it notes by me so I could write down all the thoughts that entered my mind, as it struggled to get into the open mode, about decisions I had to take. This was done in the hope that, if I wrote them down, I could then forget about them. It didn't work for me. I found that the very act of recording them gave them legitimacy. However, they should not be given legitimacy when they pop into your mind as you try to enter the open mode. I decided that my energies were better utilised recognising they were inappropriate, in staying calm, and in waiting until they eventually faded away and the creative process took over my brain.

One tip I will share with you about Roster is to not schedule too long a period of time to be in the open mode and be creative. I have found 90 minutes to two hours is about right. Over two hours is too long for many reasons. These include the fact that we do still have businesses that require closed-mode attention and decisions, the creative process can actually be quite tiring, and after two hours you have other bodily needs to attend to.

E is for Enhance. So often our creativity is limited by our discomfort at not having the solution to a problem, by our desire to make a choice or to take a decision. This part of the process is about patience, belief in the process of creativity and giving time, more time, and even more time, if necessary, to enhance the emerging ideas. It is about giving ideas the time to flourish, the opportunity to be considered without a rush to judgement, and protection from the threatening drive of the closed mode. The 'gold standard' here is to be able to access the child-like wonder and sense of exploration where there are no limitations, no fears and no limits on how much we can dream and create.

A is for Assurance. An assurance is a promise. The promise is that no idea will be regarded as irrelevant, unworthy or stupid. This promise attacks the very heart of the biggest potential block to innovation – the fear of making a mistake. It's important to enable complete confidence that whatever evolves from the open mode is okay, to create the child-like delight with the playfulness of experimentation and to remember that you cannot be spontaneous *within reason*. The promise helps people to really harness the innovation that lies in the art of 'What if?' If you're working individually, it is a promise you must make, and keep, to and for yourself. In group working, it is helpful to have a non-judgemental environment where everyone knows they will have an equal opportunity to contribute.

T is for The Funny Side. Seeing the funny side, being unafraid to be humorous, keeping the mood light and playful, all give access to the quickest and most effective ways of moving from the closed mode to the open mode. Often we limit the use of humour because we regard it as inappropriate when discussing important, weighty, serious matters. For example, if you are trying to radically reduce the time it takes to produce a new product, in order to slash the time-to-market and cut development time and costs – this is serious, right? Jobs are at stake, as is the very future of the company. This is about survival. This is serious. So often we confuse seriousness with solemnity. We regard humour as inappropriate in these sorts of circumstances.

It is wrong to equate seriousness and solemnity. I would argue that solemnity is the defence of the pompous and self-important, who need to protect against their egotism being punctured by humour. Humour might impact their self-image. The lack of humour is used by them to argue they are more serious, and their arguments therefore carry more weight. In reality, humour is an essential part of innovation, of playfulness, of creativity. Enabling the introduction of humour is a vital component of the process of innovation. Creativity lives and thrives on the funny side. While I have no research studies to confirm this, my experience tells me creative people are often more open to humour when working on serious topics, and less likely to be pompous and self-important. Seeing the funny side may be a little more difficult when working individually, but it is just as important as it is when working in teams. When I am working individually and want to be able to see the funny side, I find a mirror is helpful. It is not about vanity; it is a mechanism to check if I am seeing the funny side. The mirror reminds me that I should be smiling, smirking, laughing out loud. The visual evidence shows me whether or not I am being effective at accessing the funny side. ☺ or ☹ in the mirror?

E is for Emancipated. This goes to the heart of fully engaging ourselves as creative individuals and to getting maximum creativity from groups. Emancipation is defined as 'being not limited socially or politically'. So why choose this word? Let me start by linking back to the funny side. The emancipated see no limit to what is regarded as humorous on the funny side. Their humour mocks convention, attacks widely held taboos, and can be regarded as shocking by more conventional people. This is my point. True creativity lies beyond the boundaries of conventional wisdom, of the rules of society, of what we regard as normal behaviour.

The same emancipation applies in the earlier Enhance step. There should be no limit imposed by conventional wisdom on how far our ideas can be enhanced and stretched. Often when the idea is stretched as far as the absurd, new ideas and new thoughts emerge that would not have been considered within the boundaries of what is regarded conventionally as acceptable.

It is clear to me that pushing the boundaries, stretching the ideas, going as far as the absurd are actually the keys to accessing true creativity. I also recognise, particularly in group situations, that this can be a fairly daunting, anarchic and maybe even dangerous activity. Walking the tightrope that balances accessing the absurd on the one hand and moderating the impact of doing so on the other is challenging. Walking this tightrope is another learnable skill.

Having a skilled observer, facilitator and interventionist to help a group to navigate their way through this process of creativity is, without doubt, helpful. Be sure that whoever fulfils this role has the right focus. You want someone who is focused on future possibility, on creativity and on pushing the boundaries. You don't want somebody taking on this role mainly owing to their past experiences, as these may lead to a limiting framework. I have a lot of respect for mentors, but the CREATE facilitator role is not for them as their strengths derive from their previous experience. Far better to choose a skilled coach whose focus will be on you and your future possibilities. When I am going through the CREATE process individually, it's not unusual for me to do so with a skilled thinking partner, whose role is to be the guardian of the process, allowing me to focus on the content.

The essence of this chapter: Big Dreams are one of the fundamental components of transformation, and creativity is key to success. You have to push the boundaries and be bold in your pursuit of creativity. Boldness will come from creativity when you go beyond what is *within reason.* Even naturally creative people will boost their creativity when they follow the CREATE process, whether they are working alone or within a team. Creativity requires a different approach to that which we use most of the time in business. It flourishes within you when you are in the open mode, and have all the elements to support you in being, and staying, in the open mode for an appropriate period of time, in a suitable environment, with the right mind-set.

Your notes

If you wish, use this page to record the actions you will take.

Seven!

The more observant reader will have noticed that this is not the seventh chapter, despite the title. Seven does not refer to its position in the book but derives from a piece of wise counsel I was given when preparing for my first due diligence assignment. One of the keys to success for transformation programmes is the amount and quality of genuine two-way communication about the transformation. The recommendation I was given was to think about an extensive communication programme and then multiply whatever I envisaged by a factor of seven!

However, this should not mean blasting out seven times the volume of communication about your transformation than you first thought of. Instead this chapter will cover the process of communications and, importantly, the *intent* of communication. The intent should not be simply to communicate your transformation but to engage in an ongoing process of genuine two-way communication. Not only is it necessary to have a good plan to communicate out to all the relevant stakeholders, it is vital to plan how you will receive communication *back* from everybody. The success of your transformation will be strengthened if you can communicate to all stakeholders in a way that maximises involvement, passionate engagement and a sense of ownership. To do so, it is important that you communicate the *context* as much as the *content* of your transformation.

Start as you mean to go on. Communicate that there will be a transformation before you even know the detail of that transformation; communicate what it will mean and how people will be affected by it. Invite people to engage early with the transformation, to influence how the transformation and the journey will evolve, and to feel they have a stake in defining their futures. Be bold, open and honest in your communication. It really is alright to admit that you don't have all the answers and that you are comfortable with the concept of transformation into a future that is ill-defined at this point.

Devising your communications plan

Having a communications plan is a vital component of achieving your successful transformation. I have found a two-stage approach to be best. I use the first stage to support the creative generation of ideas about what should be communicated and the second stage to formalise this.

In order to encourage innovation, creativity and wide participation, keep Stage 1 as loose and unstructured as possible. Have a look at the process I use to encourage creativity in the *Get Creative!* chapter. Here, I want to focus on how the outputs from the creative process, that is the communications messages, are captured and structured in a way that supports the necessary level of genuine two-way communication.

The communications messages generated during the creative process simply need to be captured in some way. Personally, I throw them all into a basic spreadsheet, capturing all the messages in one column. I then create three or four columns to the right-hand side of these messages which can be used to classify the messages by urgency or importance, to add any prerequisites that need to occur before the message becomes appropriate to be communicated and to identify when the communications message has been transferred from the spreadsheet into Stage 2. Keep the Stage 1 file as a live, constantly evolving document which you update as soon as you think of something that you want to communicate. Use it to colour-code any feedback that you want to respond to, even if you don't yet know how to respond to it. The best way to kill the feedback that you so badly need is not to respond at all. Unsurprisingly, responding to feedback promotes the development of the desired ongoing process of communication.

Stage 2 is a little more formal. Again I do this in a spreadsheet, which I call the **Communications Plan Template** and this is available from the website as one of the bonus materials. This time, for each message, 11 columns need to be completed and are described briefly below.

1. First identify both the internal and external target audiences for the communication. It could be that the message is aimed at the whole internal organisation, or at a subset or even at a single individual. These three categories (whole, subset and individual) apply to external audiences in the same way.

2. Within the target audiences there are likely to be specific people to whom the message is addressed. Even a message to everyone may need to be formulated in a way that communicates directly with different groups within the whole. For example, a message to everyone in your business will also have to take account of different groups of people such as sales, finance and customer service personnel. Remember to also consider how you will get feedback from different elements of your target audiences.

3. My recommendation is to break down your target audiences into small, focused and distinct subsets to enable your messages to be as precise as possible in both delivery from you and feedback from them. We want to know a little more about these specific target audiences. We may want to know what their agenda is, what they think they already know, and what might be their 'barriers to action'.

4. It's important to be clear about the objectives of the communications messages. What message do you want the target people to receive? What are you trying to achieve with the communication? Are you trying to convince them, sell the benefits or remove their fears? When considering the objectives of communication, ask yourself what you are asking the target people to do differently.

5. Having thought about the objectives of the communication, it is time to consider the explicit messages you are communicating. These should be clear statements, clear requests for action, with clear timescales. But don't assume that, just because they are clear and explicit, they will be received in the way you had intended! Measurement of your communications strategy, as described later in this chapter, will enable you to identify whether or not your explicit messages have been received and fully understood.

6. Not all of the messages you wish to convey should be explicit. You also need to get the tone right in order to convey implicit messages such as 'Don't worry!', 'We have everything under control!' and 'You'll love the better world you will experience after our transformation'.

7. As you build your communications plan, the next stage is to think about the method of communication. There are many mechanisms you can use to communicate messages. For example, there are face-to-face one-to-one, face-to-face to multiples, or video messaging to individuals or groups. There are individual phone calls, audio conferences and webcasts to consider. There are print media, social media and digital media on the web that you could use. The method used should be chosen based on its suitability to convey the objectives of the message. For instance, if you are asking a particular individual to actively support one aspect of your transformation, putting that request into a newsletter or email that is sent to all employees probably won't achieve it! Personal messages require personal communications methods, so always consider the value of face-to-face individual communications.

8. As I wrote earlier, your whole communications plan needs to be designed with two-way communication in mind. Hence it is vital that you work out how you will elicit and receive feedback. Since feedback and measurement of the effectiveness of the communications are linked, it is important to decide how you will measure the effectiveness of your communications at the same time. You will be basing your measurement of effectiveness on feedback received from your target audiences. Think about how you will allow the targets to respond to your communication. Enable them to express themselves in the ways that are most comfortable and familiar to them. For example, only allowing written feedback may constrain the quantity and quality of feedback. Try to give people as many options as possible. Think about how you measure effectiveness. This can range from more complex questionnaires, to simple ☺ for 'understood' and ☹ for 'I don't get it', to free-format mechanisms with no structure to constrain the feedback. If you use questionnaires with a scale, avoid using one that allows people to sit on the fence. A 5-point scale where 1 is 'bad' and 5 is 'good' allows people to choose 3 as a middle ground. Give them an even-point scale such as:

Extremely happy	Very happy	Happy	Unhappy	Very unhappy	Extremely unhappy

9. Each communication message must have a clearly defined individual accountable for managing the communications process – someone who is responsible for ensuring that each of the columns you have completed for that message are effectively and efficiently managed and delivered. If you decide that a team is responsible for managing the process, please ensure that a single individual within the team is accountable for the success of processing that message.

10. The penultimate stage is to identify who is responsible for communicating to the target audiences and for managing the feedback and measurement processes. The same guidance applies regarding accountability across individuals and teams as outlined in point 9. Don't fall into the trap of all the messages coming from you as this indicates that you are the only one who is engaged.

11. The final stage sounds the easiest, but is not always so. This last task is to decide the timing of the communication. The reason why this can be tricky lies in the old phrase 'Events, Dear Boy. Events' attributed to British Prime Minister Harold Macmillan in the 1960s. The leaders of the world had gathered for an economic summit, but their focus was forced to turn from economics to the prospect of a previously unforeseen possible war. Planning timing is one thing; carrying out the communication of the message is another. The timing of the communication should always be subject to a decision; no communications should be sent out automatically using some pre-defined timetable. This means there should always be a last-minute review to ask: 'Is this really the right time?', 'Is the audience in an appropriate state to receive and process messages?' and 'What has changed since the timing was decided?'

Throughout the process of developing your communications plan, remember to think about the different filters people use. Work hard to form your messages in ways that attract and engage those who primarily 'feel' their worlds, those who 'see' those worlds, and those who 'hear'. Perhaps dip into the chapter **Big Dreams, Crafted Well, Engaging All** just before you start to complete the **Communications Plan Template**. Additionally, consider reading the bonus material **Elegant Communication Framework**.

The essence of this chapter: The title of this chapter (**Seven!**) was chosen so you get the quantity of your communications right. Your communications must be genuinely two-way. Remember you are aiming to maximise the amount of involvement and engagement because *a change imposed is a change opposed*. Carefully plan your communications messages, taking the time to really understand the purpose of each message and to get into the shoes of the people who will be receiving the messages. Take account of both internal and external audiences. Remember to communicate the context of your transformation as well as the content. Be clear and concise in your explicit messages, thoughtful and sensitive in your implicit messages. Be totally open to receiving feedback and challenging inputs from those interested in, and impacted by, the transformation of your business. Make your communications plan a living and constantly evolving document, driving an ongoing process of communication.

Your notes

If you wish, use this page to record the actions you will take.

Stop Selling, Start Listening

We humans like to buy, but really don't like to be sold to. Many small businesses believe that successful growth comes from chasing sales. I think this is a mistake and want to propose an alternative strategy. In the first part of this chapter, we will look at the psychology of persuasion, as outlined by Professor Robert Cialdini in his seminal book, first published in 1984, entitled 'Influence: The Psychology of Persuasion'. The second part of the chapter outlines an alternative way of having conversations with prospective clients aimed at growing your business – a way that does not involve any sales techniques.

As the two elements covered in this chapter are interrelated, interconnected and interdependent, I have chosen to present them in a single chapter so that this interconnectivity will become obvious.

'Weapons of Influence'

Cialdini set out to understand the factors that cause one person to say 'yes' to another person, and to identify the techniques that most effectively use those factors to bring about compliance. Cialdini describes his work as research into the psychology of compliance. He wanted to find out which psychological principles influence the tendency to comply with a request. Cialdini's work identified six principles, six 'Weapons of Influence':

Reciprocation
Commitment and consistency
Social proof
Liking
Authority
Scarcity

Underlying Cialdini's work are basic principles of human behaviour. So much of what we do is done on autopilot, where our actions are determined by habit, custom and practice, with automatic responses we are not even conscious of. Understanding these human behaviours opens up many possibilities to attract potential customers to your business, which are alternatives to the 'hard sell' approach. Let's look briefly at each of the six principles.

Reciprocation. The rule of reciprocation says that we try to repay, in kind, when someone else has given us a gift or kindness. If somebody does us a favour, we try to do something for them in return. If a friend buys us a birthday present, we remember their birthday and reciprocate with a gift of our own. If we are invited to dinner, we will invite our hosts for dinner at a later point. This is a very powerful principle, one that is very apparent at the time of exchanging Christmas cards. Many of you will know how the game goes – you get a card from someone you did not expect to send you a card, and you then scramble to reciprocate.

The principle of reciprocation leads to the giving of 'free samples'. The beauty of the free sample is that it is also a gift and, as such, can entice the receiver to reciprocate. Perhaps the most prevalent free sample now is 'Give us your email address and we will send you this wonderful free report'. One interesting aspect of the principle of reciprocity is the tendency towards spiralling escalation. A small initial kindness can produce a sense of obligation to offer a much larger return favour or gift. Thus, giving your prospective clients a free gift, particularly one that has genuine worth, can induce within them a sense of obligation to return your kindness. While genuine worth is advantageous, it is not always necessary. How many times have you been given a free pen, for which you have very little use or need, and then found yourself giving a charitable donation in return?

There are many ways to enhance the power of the principle of reciprocation. Combining this principle with other techniques can be particularly effective. For instance, once your prospective client has accepted your first small gift, in return for their email address, it may be that you offer them a more valuable gift in exchange for more information about them – information that is more valuable to you than their email address. Once you have established this dialogue in the form of 'offer, accept, provide' you are starting to build a relationship with your prospective clients. This relationship gradually builds in value and, over time, increases their sense of indebtedness and therefore their propensity to buy from you.

Commitment and consistency. The next principle is that of commitment and consistency. We humans like to see ourselves as predictable, that our actions are consistent with our principles, with who we are in ourselves and with others in society. In most circumstances, consistency and predictability are valued whereas inconsistency is generally thought to be an undesirable personality trait. Individuals whose beliefs, words and deeds don't match are seen as unreliable, two-faced or devious.

Applying this principle to attracting prospective clients to your business requires you to help them connect what you are asking them to do with what they are committed to and believe in. For instance, if you know that your prospective client has previously bought organic foods, choosing to pay a premium to do so, you can deduce that they are committed in some way to organic foods. Your task then is to present your request in such a way that identifies for them that agreeing to your request is entirely consistent with their commitment to organic foods.

Social proof. The third principle, social proof, relates to our tendency to behave as pack animals. We do what others do, we want to fit in and we don't want to be seen as radically different in many circumstances. Cialdini offers a very apt quotation. 'Where all think alike, no one thinks very much.' This is another manifestation of people acting on autopilot much of the time. Often we mimic the actions of those around us unconsciously. One of the most ridiculous examples of the use of social proof is the deployment of canned laughter. Logically we know it is canned, it is not genuine and it is a device. But so often we play along laughing in unison, particularly when in group situations. We know full well that the hilarity we hear has been created artificially by a technician at a control board and not generated spontaneously by a genuine audience. We know full well that this is a transparent forgery. Yet it works on us!

Applying this principle to your business involves reassuring prospective clients that doing business with you makes them part of the crowd, that they belong, that such behaviour is completely normal. One small example of deploying this principle is illustrated in the following scenario. Suppose you are a service business and you are promoting a series of workshops to attract new customers to your business. Showing the number of people who have already booked to attend your workshops on your website or, even more powerfully, identifying them by name, provides reassurance for prospective attendees that they will be joining like-minded people at your event. 'It's okay; lots of people just like you will be attending!' How about a scenario for a product business? You are about to launch a new product, having previously done some pilot testing. Again you have a website. Putting several testimonials from those who were involved in the pilot on that website will provide social proof for prospective buyers.

Liking. The next principle is that of liking. As a rule, we agree to the request of someone we know and like. Most people will be familiar with the Tupperware® party. The use of the 'Weapons of Influence' at the Tupperware party is fairly easy to identify. Reciprocity is applied by playing games before the buying begins – games that result in everybody receiving a gift. Commitment and consistency comes from each attendee being urged to describe how great the Tupperware is that they already own. Once buying begins, social proof is used to underline that each purchase is very similar to purchases made by other attendees. The genius of the Tupperware party is in the application of the principle of liking. The request made to buy the product is not made by a stranger; it comes from a dear friend of everyone in the room. She is the party hostess, who has called her friends into her home for the demonstration, providing hospitality and refreshments. Everyone knows the hostess will profit from each item sold at her party. She is their friend. She is their hostess. She is liked by them. Who could say no?

Applying liking to your business development activities involves creating the sense within your customers and your prospective clients that you and your company are genuinely likeable. You will have your own unique ways of creating this sense of liking. Every interaction with a customer, a prospective client or anyone at all who experiences your business must enhance the sense of liking. For me and my service business it is key that everything is congruent. This congruence is a recurring theme throughout the book. In marketing terms (that is after all the focus of this chapter), all your activities should enhance the sense of liking. The chapter entitled *Your Congruence is Vital* provides more information on the constituent parts that represent congruence.

Authority. The penultimate weapon of influence is authority. We are minded to do as those in authority tell us to do. If you are in the middle of a party, having a good time, and a shabbily dressed, unkempt and hesitant person tells you that everyone must leave the room, you are likely to think twice. If the person telling you to leave is a large, confident and commanding police officer, you are likely to be far more compliant, eager to depart immediately. We listen to those whom we perceive to have authority.

How do we apply this principle to our businesses? I'm not suggesting everyone should dress up in uniform to ask, or tell, people to buy from us. There are many other ways to demonstrate authority. Being recognised as an expert and an authority in your field will influence others who recognise that expertise. Expertise and niche marketing go hand in hand. It is an oxymoron to be an expert in everything, and stretches credibility to try to obtain expert status in a wide range of unrelated matters. Investing time in attaining expert status in your chosen field will yield benefits when done skilfully. Remember that expertise is claimed rather than awarded. You have to make the decision to be an expert, you have to establish the knowledge and credibility in your target area, and you have to claim expert status because no one will give it to you spontaneously.

Scarcity. The final principle is scarcity. Many businesses get this wrong. They market themselves as having infinite capability and capacity, they pursue as many leads as possible and their attitude is that they can never have too much work. The problem with this is how it is perceived by prospective clients. As a buyer, if I know that there is infinite supply, why do I need to make the decision to buy *now*? Unless I *have* to make a purchase, I can put it off because I know there will always be supply when I do actually need to buy. Any discretionary purchase can be delayed. There are so many suppliers of mobile phone contracts that I don't need to make any decisions until the point at which my commitment to my current supplier needs my attention at the end of the contract.

Cialdini tells the tale that people genuinely believe that the biscuits in a jar where just a few are available taste better than those from a full jar. Scarcity not only encourages people to decide to buy now, it convinces them that the item in scarce supply is more desirable, of better quality and brings with it a cachet of ownership that will reflect favourably on them. Find ways to emphasise the scarce nature of your goods and services. If you also manage to restrict your product or service offerings to a well-selected but limited range, this makes scarce the range of choices open to customers. I recall an example of a restaurant with two different menu offerings. Menu A had an enormous range of dishes to choose from, covering the cuisines of several countries over several pages. Menu B was a short, well-selected list of six dishes on one page. The vast majority of customers chose to order from Menu B, identifying it as less confusing and easier to choose from.

Enabling people to enthusiastically say 'yes!'

In this second section of the chapter, I offer you an alternative approach to getting the clients you really want for your business. It's an alternative seven-stage approach to them saying 'yes' to you heartily, eagerly and joyfully. The seven stages become relevant after you have attracted them to considering doing business with you by deploying the six 'Weapons of Influence'. They are considering buying from you, and so you now have the opportunity for them to say 'yes' to you and your business. Use the ALIGNED framework:

A   Assume control

L   Learn their situation and desires

I   Injuries and pains

G   Get commitment

N   Nirvana – the Well-Formed Outcome

E   Elegant solutions

D   Decide or die

Assume control

The prospective client has indicated that they want you to provide a solution, be it in the form of a product, a service or a combination of the two. They have an identified need, quite possibly a problem, that is causing them pain, and they want a professional to resolve it for them. They expect you to assume control, to take charge and to demonstrate authority and competence.

The first stage is to tell them the process that your interaction with them will follow, whether that interaction takes the form of a meeting, a telephone call or a conversation using social media (this process works with all three mediums, but is most effective face-to-face in person). Outline that you wish to fully understand what they want and their current situation. Tell them it is only when you reach a full understanding that you will be able to tell them whether you can help – and mean it! Do not have a pre-prepared solution in mind that you are looking to persuade them to buy from you. Congruence is all!

The quality of your listening in this process needs to be outstandingly high. Be prepared to not make the sale if your solution is not the perfect fit for them. You will not regret it. You want your customers to be delighted, not merely satisfied. Only delighted customers can become your fan club. In my work with clients, we have developed a range of techniques to develop, recruit and deploy our army of fans. Tell them that you will only work with them if you have a solution or solutions that are perfect for them. Tell them that you will not do business with them unless you can provide what is best for them (and mean it!). Tell them that, if there is not a 'best fit' you will try to suggest an alternative other than you or your company – so they know the conversation will not be entirely wasted if you don't do business together, and so they know you care.

This first stage will sound almost like a monologue from you. This is because you are taking control, as expected. While it resembles a monologue, there are two elements that will ease the process and build confidence within your prospective client. First, make it very clear that they have your full attention, using body language. Direct eye contact is key, demonstrating your sincerity, integrity and commitment. When you tell them that you genuinely don't know if you can help them until you have fully understood, look them straight in the eye if it is a face-to-face meeting. As Shakespeare and others wrote: 'The eyes are the window to the soul'. Let them see into your soul, to experience who you are and what you stand for. If you are talking over the phone, make sure your pitch, pace and tonality fully convey your sincerity. If it is a video conference, look straight into the camera lens, not at their image on the screen. If you are not sure of the impact, check it out with someone over Skype™ – the difference is dramatic. Doing this takes practice, but it is a learnable skill.

The second element that eases this stage is the words that you use. It is a monologue that you should practise many times to perfect. Practise it with a friend or colleague, and record it so you can play it back and learn from it. Your monologue is designed explicitly to outline the process. The implicit messages are just as important, if not more so. You are demonstrating your sincerity, integrity and commitment. Make explicit your commitment to the person receiving the monologue – 'My commitment to you is ....' (Mine is 'My commitment to you is to enable you to be the best you want to be'.) Implicitly demonstrate your commitment to them by focusing your language on them. For every use of the words 'I', 'My', 'Mine' and 'Our' (where it refers to your company, not to you and the client), there should be at least one 'You', 'Your', 'Yours'. Use the 'rule of three' technique from the *Elegant Communication Framework* bonus material to establish a pattern with regards to their name. Using their name once can be seen as an accident, twice as a coincidence and three times as a pattern that shows you know their name. When you listen to the recordings of your practice attempts, play 'word bingo' to measure the balance between words referring to you and words referring to them.

Analyse how well you used the *Elegant Communication Framework* in developing your conversation.

Learn their situation and desires

You know your prospective customer has identified that they want a solution, but you don't have enough information yet. It may be that they don't have enough information yet either. The ALIGNED process is designed to enable both of you to really understand what the ideal solution would be. The process of jointly identifying the desired solution, the full benefits it will bring, and the pain it will take away is the basis of building a strong and mutual commitment to a solution. If the process leads to a mutual understanding that you cannot provide the best solution on this occasion, you will still have built a stronger relationship which may deliver benefits later.

It may be that your prospective customer hasn't given the time to really think through the result they really want. If they had a magic wand, how would they use it? If their wildest dreams came true, how would that be for them? Encourage them to remove all the practicalities that might limit their imagination about what they would really want. Allow and encourage them to dream big. (It might be good to review the chapter *Big Dreams, Crafted Well, Engaging All* so you can help them dream more effectively.) Your focus should be on connecting them with what they would really like to hear, see and feel (and possibly taste and smell) in the future. Do not rush here; rather let them build and build and build. Make sure you are really listening. Clear your mind of any other thoughts than what they are telling you through their words and body language. It is important to use the exact words they use as it really demonstrates you are listening and understanding as if you were in their shoes, and not translating their words into your language. Subtle matching of their body language is also useful, if it remains imperceptible.

While building their Big Dream with them, tease out what they have tried and what the results have been. At this stage, don't go into too much detail in establishing their problems; and keep well away from presenting, or even formulating, your solution. Focus on them and what they want. Focus on building the rapport and relationship you have with them. Focus on being interested and curious. The quality of your listening will improve the quality of their thinking. Really! Try it.

While building their Big Dream with them, tease out what will become possible for them when their Big Dream becomes reality. What is the value to them? Again, build this value with them. If they could solve this problem, how would their lives be? Don't just focus on the removal of problems; allow them to describe what positive things they could be doing instead. For example, they might have a problem with the number of great conversations they have with their customers that don't lead to the customer ordering from them. They feel they waste too much of their time in those conversations. If they could solve that problem, they would not only save wasted time (the problem) but they would also make more sales (value to them). This means they would make more profits (value). That would mean they could have a less stressful time in their business (value). A less stressful time would mean more quality time with their loved ones (value). They would be a better parent (value). They would feel good about themselves, they would be seen as successful and others would envy their quality of life. (I hope you get what is going on here – a process of identifying and building value to them.)

While building their Big Dream with them, express things in the positive and, by modelling this positive outlook, encourage them to also express things in the positive. Their statements of what they want should be positive, not negative. Negativity can, and will, come later. In this part of the conversation you want to emphasise movement *towards* a positive goal with high value, not movement *away* from a problem.

When they are finished building and describing their Big Dream(s), summarise and recap using their words and phrases. Ask them if they think you have expressed things exactly as they intended. Don't rush, don't overly summarise and *do not* destroy the value you have created through having taken the time to build value, by helping them to express what they truly want. You have taken the time and considerable effort to understand them, so let them have the opportunity to appreciate your efforts.

Injuries and pains

Your prospective customer now has a very clear grasp of what they want, and what the value of having it is to them. At the moment, though, they have neither the solution nor the value. So it's time to connect them with their injuries and pains. The principles in this stage are the same as in the previous stage. The quality of your listening will affect the quality of their thinking. Listen and understand their pain(s) and don't let any part of your brain start working on solutions. Build the value with them – albeit negative value this time. Try to understand not only the symptoms but also the impact. Understand they are wasting time (how much?) in unproductive conversations with prospective customers, but also understand the pain of not spending enough quality time with their loved ones as a result. Do *not* do what I just did: I went from wasted time to insufficient time with their loved ones in one step. Tease out all the intervening steps (they don't have enough sales, they don't have enough profits, they don't have a stress-free life and so on). Build the (negative) value – their real pain.

Your language and body language again need to demonstrate your sincerity, empathy and compassion. Do not diminish your focus on their pain by starting to think about your solutions! Instead give them your time and full attention, and allow them to see that you understand both their pain and their Big Dreams equally.

Take time to understand what they have tried in the past. Be curious not judgemental, as judgement will conflict with building empathy and rapport. Remember to acknowledge their partial successes as their failures are part of their pain.

Get commitment

Now find out how much your prospective client would like to change their current world of pain. Will they make the sacrifices needed to move from what they have tried in the past to the wonderful world that will exist when they realise their Big Dreams? The sacrifices may be in the form of financial outlay, changes of behaviour or working with different people (including you) in the future.

Be specific when asking how committed they are. Use questions such as: 'In order to realise your Big Dream of ... (use their exact words), how committed are you to absorbing the pain it will take, on a scale of 1 to 10?' Don't be judgemental about their rating, but do challenge their responses to reveal their level of passionate commitment. A rating of 7 or less probably means they are not sufficiently committed. If they answer with an 8 or 9, ask them what would be needed to make them change their answer to a 10. If a client answers quickly with a 10 (or 11 or 12), I will mildly challenge with a gentle 'Really?' in order test the veracity of it in their minds.

Check they have the necessary power to deliver on their commitments, or can get that power. Help them understand what they can control and what is outside their control. But neither of you should assume that they will be limited by the confines of their span of control. Just because something is not within their direct control does not mean that thing cannot be changed in favour of their Big Dream.

So now you are at the point where they really, really, really know what they want. They really, really, really know their pains. They really, really, really are committed to the solutions. They just don't yet know what the solutions are. Nor do you, if you have truly been focused on questioning and listening, and on building rapport and empathy.

Don't worry if you have had a fleeting thought about the solution which you had to extinguish to get back 'on task'. The ability to focus on the task is a learnable skill that comes with practice. Even when you are very skilled at staying 'on task', the other-than-conscious mind will occasionally fire a random thought about the solution into your conscious mind. Just get your conscious mind to banish it.

Nirvana: the Well-Formed Outcome

The next logical step is to build the Well-Formed Outcome with your prospective client in order to create their nirvana, their state of perfection. The Well-Formed Outcome is the **Big Dream, Crafted Well, Engaging All**. Refer back or reflect on the chapter of that name. Again, building the Well-Formed Outcome with potential clients is a learnable skill that improves with practice. Remember to get them to express their Well-Formed Outcome using all of their senses – hearing, seeing, feeling, tasting and smelling.

Over time, you will form your own unique and congruent way of building the Well-Formed Outcome with prospective clients. I am deliberately not giving you the words, questions and interventions that work for me as these are only congruent with me. You must find a way of building the Well-Formed Outcome with prospective clients that is congruent with you. (The chapter entitled **Your Congruence is Vital** is pertinent here.)

At the same time, help your prospective client to discover those things that might stop them going ahead. It is far better to recognise these things at this stage. The more skilled you are at building the Well-Formed Outcome, the more committed your client will be to getting around the obstacles that could prevent them achieving their Big Dreams. The bigger the Well-Formed Outcome, the more trivial the potential obstacles seem to the client.

When you and the client have finished building the Well-Formed Outcome, summarise and reprise it, playing their exact words back to them. Tell the client you think you have fully understood everything. If there is anything at all that you are not totally clear about, resolve that lack of clarity with the client now. Don't be tempted to proceed based on the 90% you do understand. You must be congruent here – if you have not really understood it all, you won't be able to decide whether or not you can provide the perfect solution that will truly delight your prospective client and enable them to attain their Well-Formed Outcome. When you are certain you have understood it all and are ready to decide, question them to find out whether they think that you have understood everything. It is important for you to *obtain their permission* to decide whether or not you have the perfect solution. I might ask questions such as 'Are you as sure as you can be that I understand?' or 'Is there any doubt in your mind?' When you have their permission, you can move to the penultimate and most important stage. Only now are you finally freed from the confines of staying on task, focusing on them.

Elegant solutions

Pause to explain briefly what will happen next. You are going to take a moment to consider everything that has been discussed and will now, for the first time, think about whether or not you can provide the solution that is the best for them. Remind them of what was discussed right at the beginning of your conversation with them – that you will only have them as a client if you have the best solutions for them, and that you will try to find an alternative if you and your company do not have the best solutions for them. At this stage, I may choose to also remind them of my commitment to them (that is, to enable them to be the best they want to be).

Now take some time to weigh up everything you now know. Be creative in building your possible solutions for them. Don't just trot out in your mind the 'same old, same old' for you to consider using. Honour and respect your prospective client by diligently answering the questions 'Can I provide the perfect fit?', 'Can I truly delight them as a client?', 'Can this client become one of my fans?' Ensure your solution is elegant in form, that it enables them to achieve their nirvana and that it addresses any barriers to success you discovered earlier. This is the most important moment in determining whether they will say an enthusiastic 'yes' to you.

In crafting your solution, give them what they want or graciously decline their business. It is time for a congruence check before you outline your proposed solutions. Are you absolutely certain you are the best fit? Have you truly taken into account everything you know? On a scale of 1 to 10, how certain are you?

If you rate 10, then it's time to present your proposed solution. *How* you present your proposal must be congruent with you, so you must develop a way of presenting it that shows your genuine sincerity and your congruence. This is another learnable skill.

What you present should cover your proposed solution, how it will solve the problem and what consequences it will have for your prospective client. Bear in mind your 'Weapons of Influence' when presenting your 'what'. For example, emphasise the scarcity of the totally bespoke solution you have crafted and honed for them alone, if that is what you have done. Explain how the Well-Formed Outcome will be achieved, what life will be like for them as a result and the value they will get, from the least valuable to the highest. (In our previous example, that would be everything from saving time in unproductive conversations, through more sales and more profits, and everything else leading to the more highly valued quality time with their loved ones.) You should also cover the pain that will be taken away and the value that will be created for them as your client. You should outline how your solution elegantly avoids any of the potential obstacles identified earlier. Outline your proposal using appropriate and collaborative language ('you', 'your', 'our', 'we' and so on).

Don't rush when presenting your solution. Make sure you do so at a pace that is comfortable for your client. Remember to match their words and their body language. Allow them sufficient opportunity to assimilate your solution so that it can become your joint commitment. Then ask if they think they fully understand the solution and the consequent impacts on their pain (using their words) and the value that will be created for them (in their words). If they indicate they do fully understand, and you agree that they do, tell them you know they understand. Specific and explicit agreements should be verbalised, honoured and celebrated.

Decide or die

By this I mean that the prospective client should make a clear 'yes' or 'no' decision. As the professional, you should confidently ask for a decision. Don't permit the option of thinking about it because, if you allow them to defer their decision, the opportunity is dead to you. Mourn if you must, but move on elegantly, having built a greater connection with your prospective customer. You have had the opportunity to deploy effectively several 'Weapons of Influence'. You should have used all six of them in a very skilled and engaging way. You will have strengthened the person's propensity to buy from you in the future.

There is no right or wrong here, just reality. There is no failure here, only feedback. If they say 'no' you won't waste time chasing the currently unachievable, but you will have strengthened a relationship. In my experience, a 'no' can turn into a subsequent 'yes' without me expending any more effort.

By doing your job well, you have substantially improved the likelihood that they will enthusiastically say 'yes' to you. They will be so enthusiastic that they will become a fan and want to tell others about how great their experience has been. In this case, remember to celebrate! (See the chapter entitled **Celebrate!**)

The essence of this chapter: Stop selling! Stop trying to sell your predefined solutions, start attracting customers to you and start listening with intensity to those you attract. Be congruent in developing your solutions for them based on their specific situations. Don't try to match your pre-defined offerings to an approximation or interpretation of what they want, the pain they are currently experiencing, and the value they would really like to access. Be congruent, let them fully experience your congruence, and only provide what is the perfect fit for them. You don't want customers who are merely satisfied. You want an army of fans to help you achieve your Big Dream, your transformation, and the value you want to access for yourself and for those you hold dear.

Your notes

If you wish, use this page to record the actions you will take.

Organise!

Studies have shown that the majority of change and transformation programmes do not achieve the objectives originally set. The good news is that the organisations who are best at delivering transformation programmes achieve around 80% of their objectives. In contrast, the organisations who are worst at delivering change programmes deliver only 8% of their outcomes. So what can you do to improve your chances of success?

Making bandwidth for transformation

Experience working with a range of organisations to design and deliver transformational change has taught me the importance of creating a so-called 'shadow organisation'. Too many organisations assume there is sufficient 'white space' within their organisation to deliver business-as-usual everyday activities as well as the additional activities needed to bring about transformational change. In reality this is rarely the case. It is important that organisations carve out the necessary resources to enable the additional transformational activities to take place.

This does not mean that a separate organisation should be created, one that is disconnected from the real world of 'business as usual'. This is why I use the term 'shadow organisation' as there has to be a level of connectivity otherwise those delivering business-as-usual activities are likely to feel disengaged and misunderstood.

If the transformation programme has sufficiently worthwhile and desired outcomes, logically the allocation of these additional resources should not be a problem. In reality, it usually is problematic because reallocating resource often involves trying to battle overwhelming inertia. Clearly business-as-usual activities must continue. Equally clearly, if the transformation objectives are to be achieved and within a reasonable timespan, resource needs to be dedicated to these additional activities. The logical conclusion is that either the organisation needs to bring in extra resources or it needs to curtail some current activities. These difficult decisions are essentially a matter of prioritisation.

If you are reading this chapter and thinking it does not apply to you because your business does not employ many (or any) people, let me help you focus on your situation. Are you assuming you have enough 'white space' in your personal schedule? Do you really? I doubt it. Make a commitment as to how much time per day or per week you will dedicate to your transformation. Measure your ability to meet the promise you just made to yourself. The transformation of your business is important to you. Focusing on your transformation requires your time. Later in this chapter, I will outline how, *without staff*, you can create the structures that are vital to the success of your transformation.

To increase your chances of success, I want to cover three things relating to organisation. First, I explain the roles of change and their functions. Secondly I will outline how to establish the different projects that, when combined, make up the overall transformation programme. (This chapter is purely about organisation, not the nature of the transformation programme.) The final element of organisation is to look at how the projects interact, how that improves the involvement of a wider range of people, and how it increases engagement.

The roles of change

I think four distinct roles are necessary to bring about transformational change. Possibly the most important role is the role of the Sponsor. The other roles are those of Project Managers, Advocates and Targets. If you are the only person in your business, you are likely to be undertaking all four roles. If this is the case, remember that there will be Targets other than yourself whose behaviour you want to change such as partners, suppliers, customers and prospective customers.

Sponsors. The role of the Sponsor is very important. The role refers to the individual or group who has the power to sanction or legitimise change and transformation. Sponsors think about the potential changes facing an organisation, and assess the risks and opportunities that these transitions bring. Sponsors decide which changes will happen, communicate the new priorities to the organisation and provide the proper reinforcement to ensure success. Sponsors are responsible for creating the environment that enables these changes to be made on time and within budget. It is important that Sponsorship of the different projects is spread across a range of individuals, otherwise the transformation programme can look like the pipedream of just one or a few individuals. In some instances there needs to be a delegation of the Programme Sponsor's power in order to broaden the range of people involved in sponsoring the changes at the project level.

If you do not employ many, or any, people, you must carefully consider your role as Sponsor as you still have stakeholders. You must provide sponsorship for them with respect to your transformation programme.

Project Managers. The Project Managers are responsible for planning and delivering the changes, the individual projects, that create your transformation. Their success depends on their ability to identify and deal with potential problems and to manage the changes effectively. Project Managers who possess the right skills are crucial to the success of any project.

Advocates. These are individuals or groups who want to achieve a change but lack the power to sanction it. The power lies with the Sponsors. Advocates are often the opinion leaders of the organisation, or the future opinion leaders, with the ability to influence and advocate the necessary changes. They are special people and should be recognised as such. It is vital that they are engaged in the nature of the transformation and enabled to influence the design of the transformation, thus leading to enhanced feelings of ownership. Advocates should be selected carefully as they need the skill to be able to gain support from the appropriate Sponsors, since they have the power to approve the Advocates' ideas.

Targets. Targets are individuals or groups who must actually make a change. I use the term 'Target' because these people are the focus of the change effort, and play a crucial role in the short- and long-term success of the projects. To increase the likelihood of success, they need to be educated to understand the changes they are expected to accommodate, and they must be involved appropriately in the implementation process. As with Advocates, their involvement in the design will help to improve engagement and ownership.

At different times different people will play different roles. In one context they may be a Sponsor, in another a Target or a Project Manager. The issue is not whether you are Sponsor or a Project Manager, but in which type of situation you will be a Sponsor and what circumstances you will be a Project Manager. It's not unusual for people to say 'I'm a Project Manager for my boss but the Sponsor of the change to my people'. All four roles will benefit from high levels of engagement, genuine two-way communication and training to provide the skills necessary to be successful in delivering their functions.

The structures of change

Let's now turn to the structures that need to be created to enable your transformation programme to be successful. By their nature, most transformation programmes have a degree of complexity associated with them. Most are made up of a collection of interrelated and interdependent projects. The design of the programme, the make-up of the projects within the programme, and the detailed Work Breakdown Structures (created by the Project Managers) of each of the projects are all very important. There are very few worthwhile shortcuts here.

The design phase

The design phase puts a large strain on the organisation, particularly on the overall Sponsor of the programme. The Sponsor needs vision and imagination, a willingness to sacrifice and an understanding of the complexity and the impact of the programme. The Sponsor is also accountable for widening and deepening levels of involvement and engagement for everyone who will be impacted by the changes.

I am a great believer in designing programmes for today's needs, with an understanding that the needs of tomorrow may be slightly different. There must be some degree of flexibility to take account of unexpected circumstances. The analogy I often use is to refer to the direction of travel as opposed to a specific end-point. For example, 'Our first steps should be towards Africa' instead of 'Our destination is the Cape of Good Hope'.

Individual projects

Each of the projects that make up the transformation programme should have a Sponsor and a Project Manager committed to them. Remember that the Sponsor is the individual with the power to sanction or legitimise change while the Project Manager is the individual responsible for planning and delivering the changes.

The identification of the projects that make up the programme is a collaborative exercise. Project Managers are instrumental in both this process and in the subsequent identification of the Work Breakdown Structures of their projects.

The formality or informality of the project process should reflect the style of the individuals involved and also that of the overall organisation. I'm a great believer in using whatever works well, whether that is constructing checklists and monitoring progress on a scrap of paper or using detailed project management software. Nevertheless, the overall programme Sponsor will need to find a happy medium for the level of formality of monitoring and progress reporting of projects to facilitate cooperation between projects. This is where the overall Sponsor really has to focus on the team aspects, on collaboration and on collective effort and results.

However, I think there are two essentials that all projects should have and should publish – a vision statement and an objectives statement. The vision statement is how things will be when the project is complete. The objectives statement details a series of deliverables that are measurable and provide the yardstick to identify when success has been achieved. Both statements may change as time progresses, with perhaps the objectives changing to a greater extent.

Once the project's Sponsor and Project Manager have produced the vision and objectives statements for their project, and all the other projects have done so too, then it is time for the conversations to begin. The interrelated and interdependent nature of the projects means that each will require deliverables from other projects and will also be required to make deliverables to other projects. These interdependencies lead to a complete entity, rather than a series of isolated silos.

Sponsors of transformational change must show vision, empathy and sensitivity regarding the amount of pain the transformation can cause. They must demonstrate a willingness to sacrifice and to offer consistent support. If the right project and programme design, appropriate processes and procedures, and sufficient skill levels are in place, the chances of being in the top performing organisations that deliver 80% of their objectives are greatly increased.

Structures of change for a lone operator

I promised earlier in this chapter that I would outline how you create the structures to support your transformation where you are without staff. You may think that structures aren't required because it's just down to what *you* do or don't do but I am certain that, without structures, you are very unlikely to be successful with your transformation. Remember, while you may not have any staff, you do have people who can help you put the structures in place.

Changing behaviour. First you can assure your success by changing your behaviour. You get what you focus on, so focus on your transformation. Take time out to 'dream big' and craft your dreams well. Look again at the chapter *Big Dreams, Crafted Well, Engaging All.* Be ruthless about allocating time to do what is needed to support your transformation ('the important') at the expense of what is needed (often by others) right now ('the urgent'). If you don't dedicate the time, you won't succeed.

Planning. A goal without a plan is just a wish. Take the time to develop the plan and to share it with others. Involving others, sharing your plans, making sure they are engaged and committing yourself publicly is the first step in widening your circle of support. Don't commit to them things you don't intend to deliver, and ensure you deliver for them and for yourself. Take your commitments seriously, for they are how people will judge you, your credibility and your worth. It's okay to make small commitments initially to build their confidence in you and your trust in yourself. As you deliver on the small commitments and confidence grows, make more stretching commitments. Get other people to hold you to account and to share the responsibility for this so that it is no longer only your burden.

Communicating. Regularly communicate your progress and your successes to a wide range of people. Invite suggestions, comments and questions from them and respond to their inputs. If you don't get input from people initially, keep communicating, involving and engaging. Don't give up: the support network you create will help you to deliver your transformation. Find as many ways as possible of creating a shadow organisation of people around you. They may not work for you, but they are resources that you can use to support you in your transformation. They will make it feel less of an individual burden on your shoulders alone.

Recording. Keep a *daily* journal or log of everything that has gone well in your transformation. Once a week, review your record of what has gone well and identify the top three things of the week. Once a month, pick the highlight of the month. Tell your wide circle of contacts what has gone well, either on a weekly or monthly basis. Reward your progress with treats for yourself and try to do so in a way that involves others.

Meaningful consequences

I have covered the roles of change, the establishment of projects that make up the overall transformation programme and the organisation required to manage these projects and their interdependencies. The final element of organisation that I want to cover is the organisational impact of success and failure by those involved in each of the projects and in the overall programme.

There should be organisational consequences as a result of the performance of those involved in delivering the individual projects that constitute your transformation programme. Basically, those who are successful in delivery should be rewarded and openly praised. There should be a longer term impact for those who perform successfully in support of your transformation in any of the four roles and in other ways. It is good practice to make this reward openly visible (although with appropriate sensitivity if the reward is financial).

Equally, poor performance should lead to an organisational impact, although this should be done more in one-to-one situations and not publicly. Where performance is poor, it is necessary to understand the causes; lack of knowledge, lack of training or an unforeseen circumstance should be treated differently to poor performance caused by a lack of will. Where poor performance is caused by lack of will, other techniques can be deployed. The chapter entitled **Expect Setbacks** will help you with this area of managing consequences.

The essence of this chapter: Putting in place the structures to design and implement a transformational change is pivotal and will significantly improve your chances of success. Not doing so will almost certainly lead to failure to deliver your desired outcomes.

When you are transforming an organisation with other people involved, the right shadow organisation must be created, including the four role types. Thoughtful design of your overall programme, and the projects that are the constituent parts of the whole, is the way to ensure you achieve all the goals of your transformation. The agreement of interdependencies between projects, how they will be delivered and appropriate monitoring and risk management mechanisms will ensure a coherent programme, and the avoidance of silos.

When you are transforming your business, and you are the only person in the business, remember that you get what you focus on. You must be ruthless in creating the 'white space' within your schedule necessary to concurrently manage day-to-day business activities and those actions necessary for you to transform successfully.

In both circumstances, all your activities should aim to maximise the engagement of the widest range of stakeholders.

Your notes

If you wish, use this page to record the actions you will take.

Congruent Elephants and Other Creatures

This chapter will enable you to address all the Elephants in the Rooms of your small business, whether they are Red, Yellow or Plaid Elephants. This chapter will show you how to address the Yellow Polka Dot Elephants, the Steel Elephants and the Sepia Elephants. No matter whether your Elephants are rampant rebels, quiet assassins or fecklessly uninterested. No matter whether they are Elephants you have lived with for a while without challenging them or past conquerors of your valiant efforts to defeat them. No matter if they are Elephants that other people believe exist but you are uncertain. This chapter will give you the ability to address all of your Elephants and help you to enable all the other creatures in your world to be congruent. It is not only about Elephants Dancing, you want the other creatures to Dance too.

I want to be clear that you cannot directly change the behaviours of other people. And other people cannot change your behaviour. Only you can do this. What others do may have some influence on your behaviour but, ultimately, you choose how to behave *if* you are consciously self-aware. The issue of whether we are consciously aware, or whether our behaviours are determined by our other-than-conscious minds, has been discussed on several occasions in this book.

So this chapter provides a range of interconnected solutions that you can use to help other people bring about their own behavioural change. Just as in the chapter **Your Congruence is Vital!** you came to understand how to achieve alignment in yourself, in this chapter you will learn how to help others achieve their alignment.

Just as your self-alignment is vital, it is vital for other people to achieve alignment. In many ways, what you learned, and hopefully put into practice, as a result of reading **Your Congruence is Vital** is what you need when getting your Elephants and other creatures to Dance. They need congruence in order for them to Dance and they need alignment at all the logical levels. (Maybe review the bonus material **A Model for Alignment** and think about what alignment would be for your stakeholders.)

This is a good point to ask you to think about the individuals that make up your community of Elephants and other creatures. If you employ people, think about what it would be like for them if they were aligned. Think also about other stakeholders – clients, suppliers and potential clients. If all your stakeholders, be they currently Elephants or other creatures, were aligned to your transformation, how would that be?

Remember that the Well-Formed Outcome, the Big Dream of your transformation encompasses the 'why'. It is important that people understand, and can align to, the overriding sense of purpose that is the basis of your transformation. Just as customers buy the 'why' of what you do more than the 'what', your stakeholders want to align with the 'why'. A dressmaker who emphasises that she makes dresses is simply a dressmaker. She becomes far more powerfully attractive when she explains the fact that she spent 20 years feeling uncomfortable in clothes that didn't quite fit right, when she explains the resultant discomfort, embarrassment and lack of confidence, when she explains that many people suffer from the same predicament. People can more easily align once they understand why she makes dresses and can explain her motivation to others.

Choosing which Elephants to Dance with

Before addressing how to get your Elephants to Dance, I want to outline some potential consequences of trying to do so. Not all of your Elephants will want to Dance with you.

Helping them to recognise this is a very good thing for you. You need people who are as passionate about their versions of your transformation, your Big Dream, your Well-Formed Outcome as you are. Note well that I use the phrase 'their versions of your transformation'.

We are all individuals, we have our own individual Big Dreams, we have our own individual overriding sense of purpose and we have our own individual transformations. For your transformation to be successful, you want people to have individual versions of each of these three that are compatible with yours, that can be aligned with yours even though they won't be exactly the same. Sometimes the end points of your journey and theirs are the same, but their route to that end point is slightly different. It is their journey and your role is to support them in making it because their destination is the same as yours. As long as their journey is aligned to yours, is compatible with yours, then that is fine. What would not be fine is a journey that ends up at the same destination, but does so in ways that are incompatible and misaligned. For example, if your destination is to be the number one supplier in your chosen market and your values mean that you wish to achieve this position through ethical actions only, then you need others to undertake similarly ethical journeys. A stakeholder undertaking a journey to number one based on stealing patented information from a rival supplier would not be compatible for you.

Of course not all Elephants can dream either; it's extremely rare to find Sepia Elephants or Steel Elephants with dreams. Don't waste your energies trying to kindle dreams within them, just move them along to somewhere else. This process of sorting out those who can and those who cannot align with your transformation has to be done and done well. It is necessary. As you do it, remember to be a role model of alignment and do it in the right way for you, in the way that demonstrates your alignment to everybody.

A key role for you is helping those who cannot actively align with your transformation to move on to pursue their own Big

Dreams elsewhere. You must first achieve your own congruence before you can identify these incompatible stakeholders.

After this you will be able to focus on those remaining who are valuable to you and your transformation. You will then be in a position to enable the congruence of others with your transformation – but be prepared to redo some of the work you have done on your own congruence. In having conversations with your stakeholders about your transformation, make sure you deploy active listening. Your transformation should not be a rigid imposition. Remember, a change imposed is a change opposed. 'My way or the highway!' doesn't work in the long term. Try to really 'get into their shoes' to find out what they see, hear and feel as you explore your transformation together. Try to enhance your own understanding of your transformation as a result of these stakeholder conversations, building a mutual understanding.

Enabling others to align

At last we can explore how you can align all your other stakeholders, some of whom will be Elephants in the Rooms of your business, some of whom will not. Your role now is to give your stakeholders access to five things.

Trust
Hopes
Beliefs
Sense of purpose
Ambitions

The stakeholders have to choose to make use of these, to internalise their choices, to integrate them into their own models of alignment and congruence. These five things have to be part of their own individual Big Dreams – Big Dreams that can be aligned with yours.

I will cover each in turn. In addition, there is a useful and pertinent bonus material that you can get from the website showing how you can enable people to move along a continuum from cynicism to commitment. *From Cynical to Committed* does what it says on the tin.

Trust

Trust arrives on foot and leaves on horseback. Trust takes time to build and can easily be destroyed. The good news is that trust can be rebuilt, although I acknowledge that rebuilding trust is hard. Your stakeholders, your fans in respect of your transformation, want to and must trust you. You have to build and deserve their trust. You may regard some of the Elephants in the Rooms of your business to be cynical about your transformation. The bonus material will explain that trust is needed to move people away from cynicism. It will help you distinguish cynicism about a topic from the caricatured generality of what some may call cynical people.

I commend to you an excellent book on trust by Stephen M.R. Covey, with Rebecca R. Morrill. 'The Speed Of Trust: The One Thing That Changes Everything' has some very interesting, useful and practical models and tools that will help you understand how to build trust and how to rebuild it when necessary.

Trust begins with self-trust. You have to trust yourself in order for others to trust you. That's why it is very important that you are congruent and aligned. If you aren't, you are telling yourself at some level that there is something about you that is not genuine, is not to be trusted. If your environment, behaviours, capabilities, beliefs and values, identity and overall purpose in life are misaligned in some way, others will notice. They will recognise that something is incongruent, is 'off', is not genuine, is untrustworthy.

It is necessary to remove fear in order to build trust. This is not just so you can enable the Yellow Elephants to Dance. If there is fear inside your small business, it seeps out to your customers and prospective customers in so many visible and invisible ways. I have worked for some large 'command and control' organisations where people have feared their boss, senior management and their peers. They have feared the unknown, feared disciplinary or other sanctions, feared being demoted or promoted or losing their jobs. A significant part of their minds was focused on their fears.

Frightened people cannot be their genuine selves. Frightened people cannot be inspirationally creative. Frightened people cannot faithfully represent your brand to your customers. Fear stops people whole-heartedly committing. Fear stops people accessing playful curiosity, experimentation and learning. Fear stops people going beyond the confines of conventional wisdom.

Fear is a millstone. Fear discourages action. Fear emasculates transformation. Build trust, banish fear, fortify congruence.

Hopes

'Hope is a feeling that life and work have meaning ... regardless of the state of the world around you.' This was attributed to Vaclav Havel, the writer and dramatist, last President of Czechoslovakia and first President of the Czech Republic.

The full quotation is 'Hope is a feeling that life and work have meaning. You either have it or you don't, regardless of the state of the world that surrounds you.' If people don't have hope, it is your role to enable people to have it. You can't just give them hope, they have to internalise their hopes. But you can create the conditions that will support them in connecting with hope. You can share your hopes and dreams with them and so tap into meaning and possibility.

Cultivate and harvest that which motivates you and your stakeholders to take on the difficult journey that is your transformation together. Undertake both outer work and inner work. As 'outer work', work with your stakeholders to look at your interactions with others (such as customers) in terms of both the *context* of the interaction as well as the *content* in order to understand the full meaning and possibility. What do they hope for in this context? In terms of 'inner work', each individual can build a deeper relationship with their own particular hopes, dreams and ambitions. Each can develop a better understanding of the meaning they are making of your transformation and their part in it. Each can construct a greater commitment to what they really believe in as a cause, the *why* they will take action to support your joint transformation. Your task is to be their role model, their guide and their coach so that they can better achieve their congruence.

Beliefs

The process outlined for hopes is a good one for helping others to understand and connect with their beliefs. Having a greater understanding of beliefs enables people to really think about and challenge their beliefs. I have regularly found that people hold beliefs but don't understand their origin. This is another example of the other-than-conscious mind running the show without their conscious approval. It's not unusual to discover limiting beliefs, at which point people can be helped to substitute these limiting beliefs with more useful beliefs.

A better understanding of beliefs also creates, for the individual, the possibility of better alignment at all logical levels with beliefs. Your task again is to be their role model, their guide and their coach so that they can better connect with their beliefs and achieve their congruence.

Sense of purpose

Over time, I have discovered that working through these five things in this particular sequence results in maximum effectiveness. Looking at the bonus material **A Model for Alignment**, you might wonder why I haven't included identity in the five. I do spend time with some clients working at the level of identity but this work is very personal and so I need to have developed very strong rapport. Therefore, I suggest that it is a little less risky to go straight from talking about beliefs and values with your stakeholders to talking about sense of purpose. This can then enable a more comfortable discussion about identity.

In the chapter entitled **Your Congruence is Vital**, I commended to you the work of Daniel H. Pink. His book, 'Drive: The Surprising Truth About What Motivates Us' and an excellent animated video of him speaking on the RSA website are so worthwhile that they deserve a second mention here. You will find the bonus material **Your Purpose in Life: The Values You Hold Dear** provides a structure to help you and your stakeholders clarify your individual and joint sense of purpose.

As with hopes and beliefs, in enabling other people to achieve congruence by getting clarity about their sense of purpose, your task is to be their role model, their guide and their coach.

Ambitions

I find that a discussion with my clients about ambitions, after establishing clarity about sense of purpose, tends to give access to very practical things, provides a mechanism for focusing on specific things to be achieved and facilitates movement towards action. When you have a conversation with your stakeholders about their ambitions it enables them to recognise and be attracted to the ambition your transformation represents. I recommend that you use the same approach when aligning your stakeholders to your transformation, as you will uncover strong wishes to be a … or a …

You have the opportunity to create shared ambitions between you and your stakeholders – a great way to engage others in realising some of your ambitions. It is also an opportunity to create separate ambitions that are different but compatible. For instance, early on in my career I had an ambition to live in other countries, other cultures but I had no idea how to realise this ambition. My employer at the time encouraged staff to share such ambitions with the HR team. Sharing my ambition was one factor that led to me leaving my home country for a short-term assignment with my employer and this turned out to be the beginning of seven years of international experience, living in three different countries. Sharing my ambition provided access to very practical action – go and undertake due diligence on this possible acquisition in another country for six weeks.

In the chapter *Your Congruence is Vital* I encouraged you to develop ambitions beyond the current resources of your business and your stakeholders. Such bold ambitions will attract people who can identify with the challenges, standards and striving nature of your ambitions. They will be attracted by your boldness, your courage and your integrity. Encourage your stakeholders to do the same. You are likely to be more attracted to them for the same reasons.

As I help people to connect with their ambitions, I sometimes use one of my favourite questions: 'What would you do if you had no fear?' The results can be quite liberating. It is a question you might like to try when you think the situation appropriate, when you have sufficient rapport with the person. After all, it is a question you should ask yourself.

The five things above provide a useful framework for establishing congruence with you and your transformation in others, be they Elephants or other creatures. They are not a panacea, you will need more, but they are a solid framework. Some of the further things you will need to cement congruence in others are found in the chapter *Make It Stick!* Many are based on providing the right structures to enable those who are committed to your transformation to deliver effectively. The bonus material *From Cynical to*

Committed explains this in more detail and is another resource that you can use to gain and cement congruence in others. Use it to identify where each of your Elephants is within the model, and enable them to Dance!

At this point, I invite you to revisit your personal congruence work. Have you done enough to enable you to be successful applying this chapter? Do you need to sharpen anywhere? Remember you have to be prepared to change some things to achieve and increase alignment in others. You want alignment, not clones. But you have to be true to yourself in order to maintain your own congruence. Reconsider your work again to identify what things you will absolutely not compromise on, the things that are truly at the heart of you.

The essence of this chapter: Nobody can make anybody change their behaviour. Behavioural change comes as a result of individuals doing things differently. You only have control over your own actions, your own behaviour and the way you interact with the world around you. What you can do though is to create the conditions, the options and the possibilities that are most conducive to people acting in ways that support your transformation. These conditions must enable people around you to connect with them deeply, meaningfully, almost spiritually. You will be a guide, a coach and a role model of alignment so that others can achieve it for themselves.

The Elephants in the Rooms of your small business will only Dance if they want to. This is true of the other creatures as well. Your role is to help both groups to want to Dance. Remember that anybody from either group may choose not to Dance in support of your transformation. Your role is to help those who will not Dance with you to be aligned elsewhere, to declare their true intent and to recognise that partial, half-hearted or passive support of your transformation is not acceptable to you. It is not acceptable because it will not deliver your transformation.

Your notes

If you wish, use this page to record the actions you will take.

Celebrate!

Celebration is a cornerstone of transformation. It's important for you to celebrate achievement and also to actively seek out opportunities to celebrate, particularly in the early days of your transformation. You have probably heard the phrase 'low hanging fruit'. In this context, harvest as much 'low hanging fruit' (that is, easily achievable successes) in the early days as you can, and then take the opportunity to celebrate well and often. Many people have the attitude that once the low hanging fruit has been harvested there is no more to pick. I have learnt that, once you have picked your low hanging fruit – your early wins, your early opportunities to celebrate – providence prevails and the higher hanging fruit gravitates downwards. A second harvest can begin and celebration can continue. In my experience, this gravitational process can continue for quite a while but the resources required are usually quite modest. At the same time, I always make sure that some of my resources are focused on the much more difficult tasks that will eventually yield further bounty.

While the very phrases 'low hanging fruit' and 'easy wins' seem to suggest they deliver modest value, their value can be multiplied many times with the simple, very low cost, addition of celebration. Adding celebration brings many benefits. It produces a 'feel good factor'. It produces a shared sense of achievement. It produces a feeling of progress on the journey of transformation. The phrases may be trite, but the value is precious and transformational in itself.

If you feel there's nothing worth celebrating

There may well be times when it seems you have no successes worth celebrating, either because you think nothing has been achieved or because you think what is being achieved is inconsiderable. I have developed for my own use and for that of my clients a simple, effective and totally free way of identifying and celebrating successes.

The process is so simple that many of my clients, who follow it initially and recognise the resultant benefits, later lose focus, stop doing it and then wonder why their worlds are somehow less positive, successful and joyous. I've found myself amongst this lapsed group on more than one occasion.

The process is astonishingly simple indeed. Each and every day, allocate a few minutes to think about your day, looking for the positives in it. It helps if you build this into your routine, your schedule, your diary at the same time every day. Perhaps experiment with different times in the day, initially, to identify which time works best for you.

Each day, write down three things that have been positive about the day.

Each week, review the past seven days of positives (of which you now should have 21) and pick the three most significant, most rewarding or most enjoyable positives for that week. You can choose the criteria if you don't like my suggestions. Write them down, underline them or highlight them – whatever works best for you.

Each month, review the positives you selected in each week and pick the best three for the month. Again, using whichever method works for you, document these three highlighted positives. Keep doing this.

If you do nothing more than described in the previous three paragraphs, and keep doing it, you will get more positives. We get what we focus on. Shortly, I will give you additional activities that will add further value for you. Before I do, I want to explain what is going on in this process.

This is about your conscious mind training your other-than-conscious mind. You are taking positive action to take control of your other-than-conscious mind, which determines so many of our actions, our emotions and the results we get as a consequence. With constantly repeated iterations, the other-than-conscious mind slowly starts to 'get it'. The more you do this, the more your other-than-conscious mind begins to adopt this pattern. What is happening is that new neural pathways are being established in your brain. Over time you might think that the other-than-conscious mind would adopt this positive approach as the modus operandi or the default setting, using the new neural pathways. Despite these new pathways, the other-than-conscious mind seems to have a devilishly effective way of returning to old habits the moment you take your eyes off the ball and stop recording your positives.

As I said, I have taken my eyes off the ball and lapsed before, and it is my belief that I will do so again. Let me share what I have learned about myself, and what appears to be the experience of others too. The first part of my learning is to record the positives each and every day without exception. This means recording positives, not only when things are not going well for me and I want to cheer myself up by noticing more good things, but also recording positives when things are going well as this seems to amplify the effect of the positives.

I only came to understand this amplification when I made a conscious decision, in a very successful time, to restart recording positives each evening. My reason for choosing to restart at a time when the positives were plentiful offers some potential learning for you. When I analysed the occasions that I had lapsed I realised I only noticed that I had lapsed when things were not going particularly well. When things were great and my cup of positives was overflowing, I hadn't noticed the lapse. So here is what I offer you: When things are going really well, and your cup of positives is full, don't stop recording positives each day, each week or each month. Keep it going.

Find whatever way, mechanism or device works for you and makes it easy for you to do this work every day. Routine is important. Doing this at the same time each day emphasises the routine nature and gets you into the discipline of the daily recording of three positives.

As you do whatever works well for you, ensure the positives you identify are also expressed in positive terms: 'I completed the new page for my website' or 'I got to speak to the prospect I have been trying to reach for days' or 'My new clients just settled my first invoice'. They don't need to be momentous, ground-breaking or particularly significant. They just need to be positives that are positively expressed. They should *not* be expressed as the avoidance of a negative: 'That meeting could have gone a lot worse' or 'We haven't heard about our bid, so at least we haven't been thrown out yet' or 'We haven't lost any more customers today'.

Other activities to add value

These remarkably simple additional activities will also add value for you.

▸ Be sure to add every success into your communications plan (you may want to have a quick look at the chapter entitled **Seven!** and a glance at your current communications plan if you have already produced one.) As you communicate and celebrate your successes, remember to use a wide range of senses in your language. Paint pictures of the successes and of the ways in which you celebrate. Tell stories about them, making it clear what people said. Enthuse about how good it feels, how proud everyone is and how motivated it makes people feel. Ensure you communicate to the widest range of stakeholders, to customers, to employees and to others with whom you have connections including prospective clients, current and future partners and suppliers, and those involved in PR, media and marketing. Your communications plan provides a structure to increase the effectiveness of your messages.

▸ Take your positives and share them with others. Convey their full meaning, explain their implications and provide the context that makes them significant for you and for the person with whom you are sharing. Encourage them to share with you how they experience your positives: what they hear, what they see and what they feel. This is another opportunity for you to enable them to achieve and deepen congruence with your transformation and their individual version of it. Get this right and it is very powerful. Get it wrong and it can sound boastful, shallow and disengaging. Think through the context you need to establish, the joint understanding that must exist and the access to joint values and beliefs, and the overall sense of purpose that will increase congruence and alignment.

▸ Ask your stakeholders about their positives. Do so in a sensitive way that still enables them to moan about their negatives if that is what they need to do. Be sure to be in their shoes before seeking to move their feet to a different path. Act as a role model, a guide and a coach so that they experience the benefits of getting what they focus on.

▸ When you celebrate your successes, do so in a way that is as inclusive as possible. You may be the instigator, but you need not be the organiser. Sharing the responsibility for celebration not only widens participation, but also deepens the connection and sense of ownership and achievement. It is a great opportunity to help your stakeholders to create and enhance congruence with you and your transformation. As you participate in the celebration, be sure that your language is about what has been collectively achieved: it is more about 'we' than 'I'. Don't just think about the words you use, but also your body language and the other ways in which you communicate such as where you choose to sit, how long you choose to stay, and how much undivided attention you give to the celebration.

▸ If your celebration includes rewards ensure that, whatever the reward, it is congruent with whoever is being recognised. I remember one client introduced rewards for those whose behaviour clearly moved forward their transformation programme. That was good. What was not so great was the somewhat impersonal nature of the reward. It was somewhat impersonal because everybody got the same reward and it therefore had different value for different people. It was somewhat impersonal because it was a cash reward that was liable for taxation. Although the reward went down with the organisation very well at first, as time went by the rewards were criticised more often and a growing scepticism, perhaps even cynicism, spread across the organisation. Remember that rewarding and celebrating positive achievements is for all stakeholders, even you! Whoever or whatever the recipient, make sure the reward is personalised and congruent with them.

▶ A final warning about celebrating derives from many mistakes repeated by people in a range of situations that I have witnessed. I beseech you to be careful how you treat history. I have seen so many instances where the desire to realise the benefits associated with the future transformation has led to the achievements of the past being ignored or belittled along with the people whose efforts were associated with those achievements. I don't think that using 'The King is dead, long live the King!' works in the long run. It is far better to honour and respect the past. Certainly, don't be constrained by it, don't be a prisoner of it like the Sepia Elephant, but don't denigrate it. It was another time, another situation and you should honour it. It is distinct from now and the future you and your stakeholders are creating together. End of warning.

The essence of this chapter: Embrace the idea of picking 'low-hanging fruit' since, after you pick it, higher fruit gravitates down. You get what you focus on. Focus on your successes and they will multiply. If all your stakeholders focus on their successes, their successes will multiply. When you all focus on the successes of your transformation, they will multiply. Involve as many people as you can, as deeply as you can, creating meaning for them that allows them to be congruent with your successes. Reward people with the things they value. Reward yourself in the same way. Honour the past, don't be a prisoner of it, and don't belittle past achievements.

Your notes

If you wish, use this page to record the actions you will take.

Expect Setbacks

Setbacks are good. If you have not been getting individual setbacks, you are not trying hard enough and you are being too conservative. I will talk about setbacks which threaten the totality of your transformation later in this chapter. For now we will just look at setbacks that don't threaten the totality.

When I refer to setbacks, I include setbacks that you encounter personally and those that are experienced by your stakeholders. The most important thing, in both cases, is the reaction that follows the setback. However much effort any of you expend, there will be times when things don't go right. In the chapter **Make It Stick!** I will cover the things you can do to maximise the chances of your success and to minimise the frequency and extent of setbacks.

Use your setbacks

Any setback is an opportunity for learning. There is no failure, only feedback. People remember when things go wrong. If the setback is handled well, in a way that both recovers the situation and shows care, attention and respect, then the recovery can be more memorable that the setback.

I well remember visiting Disneyland Paris about ten years ago for a business conference. Organising a large group of about 120 people presents many challenges, and we managed to make life difficult for our hosts. When the conference room was cleared by the hotel staff at the end of the day, we realised that some notes required for the next day had been taken away when the room had been cleared. The six of us who were organising the event shrugged and went to find the soft copy to print out the notes again. You've guessed it – no soft copy. We explained the situation to our main Disneyland contact who had noticed that something was amiss and wanted to offer help. She quickly grasped that we were concerned and feeling rather foolish. With total calmness and sincerity she said, 'Don't worry, my team will find the notes for you. I'm sure of it!' I admit I had little faith in her team being able to find a couple of pages of indistinct A4 among all the rubbish and discarded papers of 120 people. Sure enough, 30 minutes later, she returned with the missing papers. I was surprised, relieved and grateful in equal measure. I managed to quell my excitement enough to ask her 'How?' With a knowing smile, she said, 'This is what we do best. When things go wrong, that is our moment of truth. That is when we really shine. When things go wrong, it is how we recover that is always remembered more than the thing we got wrong.' Although she and her team hadn't done anything wrong, her attitude was to recognise that something had indeed gone wrong and so she acted just as she would if they had been responsible.

Recovering from setbacks is more important than the setbacks themselves. Be supportive of those who fail through trying to push and test conventional wisdom. Recognise and acknowledge their intent, for it is they who have taken the risk of standing out from the crowd. It's important they know that you appreciate their efforts and their intentions. It is better to fail trying than not to try at all. Make sure you recognise effort and not just success. Too often the focus is on all-or-nothing. Praise is only given to the successful; where results are less than adequate, no praise at all is forthcoming. There are times when it's appropriate to acknowledge the efforts of those who did not quite succeed. There is still an opportunity to learn from the experience and to re-engineer future attempts, and so acknowledging the last attempt can encourage future boldness, diligence or whatever was missing. Acknowledging effort encourages further effort.

Understanding lack of support

There does come a time when a response is needed for those who consistently fail to deliver results. It's important to work out the root cause of the failure or setback. There is a big difference between someone who fails owing to lack of competence and someone who fails owing to lack of commitment. A shortage of competence is more easily remedied than a shortage of will. Those who lack the will are not those you want to share your transformation journey. You cannot duck this, you cannot buckle and you must be resolute.

I have been told that I demonstrate 'ruthless compassion' in these circumstances. I am compassionate about those who lack the will. I understand that the journey with me to our transformation may not be for them, that they have different causes they are passionate about, but I am ruthless enough to know that I have to act. Not to act sends a clear message, both to those who lack the will and to those who are still undecided.

I have seen many instances where the lack of will was concealed cleverly, where 'lip service' has been paid to the transformation, where outright dissent and opposition has been avoided but there is insufficient consent and co-operation. These can be quite tricky to manage, but they do have to be managed. Usually I will share my concerns privately with the individuals concerned, seeking to understand and being curious about their worlds. Without a clear conversation to find understanding, the situation will at best continue and at worst deteriorate. The conversation is always about commitment. If the individual's commitments are elsewhere and their consequent commitment is insufficient to support the transformation, then it is my job to bring clarity to the situation. Again, it is the behaviours not the individuals to which I refer. Ultimately, transformation needs all of the right behaviours from the vast majority of the people for the vast majority of the time.

Acting in private or in public?

There are times when I have chosen – after much careful consideration – to deploy my remedial action quite publicly, to make an example of the situation. When I choose to act in the open, and to share my views in public, I am always careful to separate the behaviour from the person. It is the behaviour that I regard as unacceptable, not the person.

There are times when action in public has to be somewhat stage-managed. Let me explain with an example. I was involved in a large scale transformation, working with a divided management team, some of who were just giving lip service to the changes. The team managing the transformation had created a sizeable change team that included senior leaders of the organisation. We had been dancing around the table with two of the most senior of these leaders, trying to understand the level of their commitment. The change team was due to undertake a five-day seminar that was designed to either make or break the transformation programme. We decided to design only the first three days of the seminar, deliberately leaving the design of the final two days to be carried out over dinner on night three so we could react to the events of the first three days.

One of those two most senior executives spent almost all of the first three days closeted with his management team, paying little attention to the activities of the seminar. This was not the sort of collegiate behaviour we were trying to foster in the company. We decided to give the executive a chance on the final day to present to the assembled group, sharing his interpretation of one aspect of the transformation journey.

This was to be a set-piece opportunity for the executive to demonstrate his understanding of, and commitment to, the transformation. We scheduled for him to kick off the final day, and let it be known that this was a very important opportunity for the executive to get behind the transformation and show solidarity with the rest of the team and the company. We allowed the executive to very publicly demonstrate that he was not committed, and he did not disappoint. Having allegedly been out on the town until the wee small hours with his management team, his commitment to the transformation programme came over as less than fulsome. His subsequent departure from the company was a very public display of the consequences of a lack of will, of a failure to publicly get behind the transformation.

We derived no satisfaction from his demise, but it was his free choice to behave in this way and he could have chosen to support the transformation. The rest of the organisation was left in no doubt about the serious nature of a lack of commitment to the transformation. There are times when this sort of public display is necessary. The general level of commitment to the transformation in the company was transformed as a result of an admittedly high risk strategy, leading to the removal of one of the most senior and capable executives. The risky strategy was pursued because it was felt that the transformation programme would ultimately fail unless the issue of commitment in the senior leadership was addressed. Eggs get broken when you are making omelettes. There are times when you simply have to address the Elephants in the Room, when you have to remove the roadblocks, when a stand has to be made. If you choose this approach, you really have to commit fully; faint-heartedness will not get it done.

The right Dancers

Mixing my metaphors, you must get the wrong people off the bus, and do it in the right way. They are wrong for your transformation but they are not bad people. They can thrive and prosper elsewhere. The important thing is to do something. Remember that imperfect action is always better than perfect inaction.

Don't be reckless, but get the balance right between the *action* of the imperfect solution and the *inaction* derived from perfecting your response before acting. Inaction lends credibility, longevity and courage to the supporters of the status quo you're trying to change. Inaction also creates uncertainty, doubt and fears in those who might be the very people who will take action to recover from setbacks.

If you don't know what to do, use my favourite management technique – MSU (Make Stuff Up). Action is better than inaction. It doesn't always have to be 'ready, aim, fire'. Sometimes the sequence is different: 'act, monitor and react' is the best way. Adopt a sensible approach to risk management, which is a state of mind as well as a series of processes. Take the hard decisions. Do so inclusively, share the load, responsibility and sense of ownership. You don't have all the answers, and sometimes they will come from an unexpected quarter. Remember you don't control as much as you think you can or think you do. As I work with clients, I accept that some of the benefits we get are attributable to neither me nor the client. Sometimes things just happen. It is amazing how often good things just turn up to help you once you have committed to something.

Whenever you have a setback, remember the chapter entitled **Seven!** It is vitally important that clear communication is established that communicates what the setback is, and what is happening as a result. You also have to be adroit in addressing any misconceptions about what the setback is or might become. You cannot *not* communicate. People will assume and interpret, so address potential assumptions and interpretations in your communications.

Sometimes people other than you will have setbacks on their journey to their personalised version of your transformation. Be as supportive as you can be for them and help them to maintain their congruence with their personal version of your transformation. It isn't always about the direct route from A to B. Sometimes a slightly more circuitous route will add meaning for them. Help them to understand that having setbacks is good, is normal and is entirely to be expected. What is important is not the setback, but how they react to it. Remind them of some of the setbacks you have experienced in order to build a greater sense of connection and the feeling of shared experiences and common understanding. Take every opportunity you can to increase their sense that you are journeying together and are being mutually supportive. Remember to be curious about their reaction to their setbacks. You cannot assume that they will react in the way that seems natural to you.

The essence of this chapter: If you don't get setbacks and disappointments, you are not stretching enough. The secret is how you react, how you recover and how you maintain congruence. Stay calm, be honest about any setbacks and take compensatory action. There is a big difference between lack of skill and lack of will. There is no failure, only feedback. Test, learn and improve. If you decide you have to take high risk and high impact action, recognise that is your choice and fully commit. You must be bold, courageous and steadfast. Take the hard decisions and engage everyone in the process. When you do, remember **Seven!** It isn't always about the shortest journey between two points. Sometimes the longer journey can impart real meaning for people, which increases their sense of ownership and commitment.

Your notes

If you wish, use this page to record the actions you will take.

Make It Stick!

The majority of transformations fail to some degree. Some fail completely or, where they don't fail completely, they don't deliver all of the original objectives. How do you make your transformation not only successful, but long-lasting? How do you make it stick?

What tends to happen in most transformations is that the original objectives are not captured and documented, and the transformation is allowed to drift. The work you have done as a result of what we have covered so far, and in particular the work of **Big Dreams, Crafted Well, Engaging All**, should have enabled you to be clear on what your objectives are. Make sure they are well documented, so that you can evaluate your progress and celebrate your successes.

I'm not saying that your objectives will never change, nor am I arguing they never should. Stuff happens, and you have to react to it. Ironically, one of the surest ways to ensure your transformation fails is to stick dogmatically to your original objectives, ignoring all relevant events that occur and becoming more and more detached from the current realities. I have been very close to a programme almost failing because of the absolute clarity (and, therefore, lack of flexibility) the business leader brought to the end point he was aiming for. It was he who brought me to tell you in the chapter **Organise!** that you should initially communicate a direction of travel to Africa, rather than a specific end point of the Cape of Good Hope.

Many people don't really understand what causes a transformation programme to be successful. It is commonly assumed that the barriers to success are the hard factors such as shortage of resources, scarcity of process and lack of equipment – and, therefore, that securing these things guarantees success. But studies have shown that the causes of failure are not generally these hard factors and that shortage of resources is only number four in the top five barriers to success:

1. changing mind-sets and attitudes
2. organisational culture
3. underestimating the complexity
4. scarcity of resources
5. lack of commitment at senior levels.

Rather, the soft factors are the most important – things such as commitment, beliefs and passion. The studies indicate that the top five drivers of success are:

1. management sponsorship
2. employee involvement
3. honest and timely communication
4. an organisational culture that motivates and promotes change
5. change agents.

This is why so much of this book has emphasised soft factors. In my experience soft factors are more difficult to get right, take longer, and are an ever-evolving, living creature. In fact, as changeable as people. That's why I have focused on soft factors.

Although soft factors are the most important, they are not enough **on their own**. So steel yourself to look at implementing process in the rest of this chapter.

Embedding your transformation with processes and systems

The hardest part of any transformation is making it stick. How you embed your transformation into the very DNA of your organisation, how you make 'business as usual' of your changes, how you get everything aligned has to be supported by the processes that you design. Once you have people's commitment, all they then need is structure. It's your responsibility to ensure that the right processes are created and followed. This doesn't mean that you have to be the designer of the processes; whether you are a lover of process, or you are process-averse, it's your job to ensure the processes to support your transformation are created, developed and kept up to date to reflect stuff that happens.

When developing your processes, it is best to adopt an iterative approach. It is far better to implement an imperfect process, and to gradually improve it, than it is to implement nothing. It's important that, whatever processes and structures are designed and implemented, they are consistent with your culture and style of operation. As long as the processes are tested to ensure you get the right results, the minutiae of the process such as how detailed your documentation needs to be, for example, can be determined by the test of 'fit for purpose'.

I have a range of modules that I work through with clients. Some of the modules are specifically designed to discover and improve the processes of the business. Every business has processes, even if they are not documented. Some businesses have several ways of trying to do the same thing. For example, it may be that a business of five people has five different ways of answering the telephone. It may sound a small detail, but what is the impression that is being created? Is the caller dealing with a professional, predictable, reliable business or five individuals doing their own thing? If each employee describes your goods or services differently, what impression does that create?

Understanding how your business actually operates is an important way of making your transformation stick because it gives you the opportunity to design things the way you want them to be. It opens up the nirvana of replicable, predictable success.

Let me give you an example taken from my experience working with a small business owner delivering personal services in a retail environment. I asked her what her ideal client would be, in terms of the mix of services she would want them to buy from her. Her response was that she would like them to take services A, B and C (the detail of the services is unimportant). Success was clearly defined as delivering services A, B and C in combination: the client would sit in a chair in her store, and the business owner would deliver the three services. I asked her how often this happened. She didn't know, but guessed at 15–20% of the time. Two pieces of learning were immediately evident – she wasn't measuring how often she was getting success and it was likely that 80% of clients were not buying her ideal combination. I next asked her what happened immediately before the client sat in her chair. With a quizzical look at me, she told me that the client was greeted by the receptionist immediately before this. I explained that I wanted to understand the client pathway that got clients into her chair, and asked her what the receptionist said to clients just before they sat in her chair. The answer was a curt 'How would I know? I am by the chair and the receptionist is way over there!'

I think you will have got the picture by now and will have guessed that, over time, the business owner and I documented the current client pathways (processes) that ended with a client sitting in her chair, but started at several different points much earlier in the process. Some clients started their journey by reading an ad in the local paper, some by finding her website after searching for local suppliers of her services, and some with a referral from a friend recommending her business. Once we had documented the various client pathways, we estimated what percentage fell off the client pathway at each stage (there were no measures in place). We then started to look at how the conversion rate from one stage to another could be improved, and modelled the impact on her revenues and profits. It wasn't rocket science; it just hadn't been done before.

The simplest things had great potential. Giving the receptionist the ability to offer clients, who had booked only one service, a 'special deal' next time they visited on a package including services A, B and C had great potential. It was actually cheaper to deliver the three services together than individually, and so the discounted package would yield higher profitability. In case you are wondering, we considered trying to upsell during the first visit rather than offering the deal for a return visit, but it would have caused scheduling chaos and impacted customer service to other clients.

Over time, we went through each different pathway, put in place measurement where we could, made some changes, and tracked the results as best we could. Some things didn't work, so we tried others, again monitoring where we could. Some patterns began to emerge. The improvement process seemed to get less onerous, even for my process-averse business owner who delegated a lot of the responsibility for documenting the processes and tracking the changes to her team. She concentrated on the bottom-line results for her business, delivering great service to her clients, recruiting them to her army of fans and rewarding them for referrals to new clients. As an outsider to her business, I thought her already great team seemed to get even more enthusiastic over time. My client was a creative person who did not see herself as 'doing process'. By involving her team, explaining what she was trying to achieve, and enabling them to share the accountability and ownership, the business created processes that were reflective of how they were as a team, their culture, and what they really stood for. Some of the changes were physical, such as slight changes to store layout and scripts to be followed in certain situations. Many of the changes were more about behaviours, about emotions and about creative passion. Over time, she managed to embed the right balance of process and creative passion, improving her business for all stakeholders.

This client needed very few systems to support her business. We focused on the processes, the steps of her business and did not see benefit in investing in systems (tools). In your business, systems may bring benefits in themselves and may improve the consistency of operating your processes. It is very important to make sure you have the right processes in place before trying to systemise your business, and to ensure the processes define the systems rather than the other way around.

The essence of this chapter: Success comes from harnessing both hearts and minds. Success comes from the blending of physical and emotional changes. Success comes from the amalgamation of intellect and passion. Once you have committed people, all the extra they need is structure. Enable them to create structure, adapt structure from elsewhere, give them structure. Your transformation needs processes in addition to the congruence, passion and sense of purpose we have covered in other chapters. Structure and processes are supportive bedrocks for your Big Dreams, your Well-Formed Outcomes, your transformation. Keep your processes and systems congruent with your culture, your values and what you are naturally comfortable with. Enable your organisation to do the same. Make the processes and systems part of the DNA of the organisation, make them 'business as usual', make them progressive. Processes and structure are not enough on their own. They support all that you have done to get congruent Elephants and other creatures to Dance.

Your notes

If you wish, use this page to record the actions you will take.

Bigger Dreams?

What happens once you have achieved your transformation and your Big Dream has come true? Is that it? Is there any more to do, to be, to learn? My somewhat philosophical view is that there is always more. My working life has always reinforced this viewpoint. I started out as a manufacturing professional and had the notion of continuous improvement (later known to me as *Kaizen*) unceasingly poured into me. In business I have been weaned on an eclectic mix of a philosophy of 'marginal gains' (as employed triumphantly by Sir David Brailsford with British Cycling) on the one hand, and the 'Come to the edge' philosophy on the other. The full quotation, attributed to Guillaume Apollinaire, the French poet, writer and art critic, is:

> 'Come to the edge', he said. They said, 'We are afraid'.
> 'Come to the edge', he said. They came.
> He pushed them ... and they flew.'

I know that, as I get close to completing any substantive task or project, I have a tendency to move on to the next, setting more stretching goals and starting new tasks and projects before completing those of the first. I recognised this early enough in my career to ensure that each of my management teams included at least two 'Completer-Finishers' (the role defined by Dr R.M. Belbin as one of the Belbin Team Roles). Their task was to ensure the last 10% got delivered while I was off starting the next journey. When it was time to celebrate completion of the original project, I would return to share the joy of my 'Completer-Finisher' midwives.

As this book reached the point at which the final manuscript was almost ready for handover to an editor, I was unsurprised to find myself drafting the outline for the next book. I recognised my new-found passion for book two and allowed myself two hours, and two hours only, to work on it recognising it as a mere dalliance that could divert my focus away from completing this book.

My point is that I suspect I will always want to set new goals once I have achieved the ones I had previously set. If you get to the point where you have achieved your transformation, or you are close enough so that you want to achieve an even greater transformation, then celebrate all you have achieved and get ready to do it all again. That's right, do it all again – starting again with **Big Dreams, Crafted Well, Engaging All** and working through the book one more time, in whatever order pleases you.

On the other hand, I am open to the possibility that I will someday say 'I'm done!' I certainly recognise the possibility that you will get to this joyous point, and I sincerely hope you do. My commitment to you is to enable you to be the best you want to be. When you get there, I want you to enjoy the achievement and the results completely. I encourage you to live fully in the moment, to experience life in all aspects. Recognise how things are for you, using all the five senses, and bask in your new-found nirvana.

When you get to achieve your Big Dream, I hope you will use all the gifts you have.

One Christmas morning an excited and breathless seven-year-old boy in red pyjamas ran down the carpeted stairs from his first floor bedroom to the lounge below, his feet making rapid dull thuds on each tread. It was a little after five-thirty in the morning; the house was dark and revealed little other than the smells of pine needles and last night's mince pies. He turned the door handle and charged through towards the Christmas tree and the pile of brightly coloured gifts that lay around the base. His breathlessness would not hold him back; he grabbed the nearest present that had his name on it and scrambled to find an unsealed edge to the red and green wrapping paper. Unsuccessful, he just tore at the paper to reveal his gift. *'Hey!!!'* he gasped. *'This is the same one as last year!!*' What was going on? He quickly found a second present and eagerly broke through the reindeer paper. '*Hey!!*' A third present. '*Hey!! HEY!!*' A fourth, a fifth! '*Hey!! This isn't right! This isn't fair!*' Close to tears, with anger and confusion coursing through him, the boy raced back up the stairs to his parents' bedroom.

Without looking to see if his parents were awake, he yelled as he rushed into the bedroom, lit by a single bedside light, '*What have you done? They're all the same as last year! Why have you given me the same gifts as last year? It's not fair!*' His mother and father were sitting up in bed as they had heard their son charge down the stairs a few moments earlier. His mother looked at him with love in her eyes and spoke with a calm, quiet and soothing voice, '*Your gifts are all the same because you haven't used them yet. Use them this year and you will get more next year.*' A devoted expression came upon her face as she added '*Share your gifts this year and you will get double next year!*'

When you get to achieve your Big Dream, I hope you will share all the gifts you have.

The essence of this chapter: Just as in every chapter of this book, in every stage of your transformation, in every moment of your life, you have choices when you get to your nirvana. I hope you make them consciously. You can choose to be in the moment, to bask and luxuriate, to really appreciate all you now have, enjoying fully your new circumstances. You have enough, you are enough, you share enough. Alternatively, you can decide to reset everything and dream even bigger dreams. If so, go back and do it all again, starting afresh with *Big Dreams, Crafted Well, Engaging All*. Whichever choice you make, I wish you well. Whichever choice you make, I urge you to use all your gifts. Whichever choice you make, I implore you to share all your gifts.

Your notes

If you wish, use this page to record the actions you will take.

Bonus Materials

Here is a list of bonus materials that you can obtain from the book's official website (www.dancewiththeelephants.com) and a chart showing the chapters for which they are most relevant. The list is as it was at the time of the book's publication. Further bonus materials will be made available over time, and the website will have the latest list. I hope you will join our community of Dancers with Elephants and submit materials you have found useful in your transformation.

Available bonus materials

- A Model for Alignment
- From Cynical to Committed
- Your Purpose in Life: The Values You Hold Dear
- Elegant Communication Framework
- Communications Plan Template

Chapters and bonus materials

Chapter	Bonus material
Big Dreams, Crafted Well, Engaging All	A Model for Alignment (Elegant Communication Framework) (From Cynical to Committed)
Your Congruence is Vital	A Model for Alignment Your Purpose in Life: The Values You Hold Dear
Seven!	Communications Plan Template Elegant Communication Framework
Congruent Elephants and Other Creatures	From Cynical to Committed Your Purpose in Life: The Values You Hold Dear

Acknowledgements

To my clients, those from my time in employment and those who have been clients of WTT Results Ltd, for sharing with me openly and honestly the challenges they faced, and for the courage to dream and take the necessary actions with me to achieve their transformations.

To previous employers and work colleagues from my time in employment, for providing me with the opportunities to learn and to gain experience – and have massive amounts of fun while doing so.

To KF and PL, my earliest guides in the world of business, for instilling in me that transformation is what business is all about.

To Sir Peter, for creating an environment where I could truly choose to be the best I wanted to be, for giving me access to 'the best of times', and for generously agreeing to write the foreword to my book.

To DFB, for being a wise and thoughtful mentor who understood and supported my personal choices, whether in agreement or not.

To MC, CAH and WVM, for guiding me to opportunities with inspiration and support. In many ways, they were, and remain, my 'gold standard'.

To RHEP, for skilfully delivering the advice to this potential bull about appropriate behaviour in a Royal Copenhagen china shop.

To a very special Profound Ocean, for bringing about an extraordinary transformation within me that was both enjoyable and painful at times.

To Serena, for providing me with the opportunity to take my first baby steps as an author, and for generously encouraging me.

To Dawn, for being a true friend and an extraordinary one-woman support system. All transformations need support systems and Dawn has been a huge contributor to mine.

To Jeanette, for being a friend indeed when I was a friend in need.

To Joolz, for inspiration and for sharing her journey in authorship with me.

To Raymond, for making the difference that made it possible to get this book into your hands.

To those who have reviewed my book, for giving their time and insights so generously.

To Tracey, for the insight that led to the discovery of the Blue Elephant in the Room, and all that evolved from it.

To Denise, my editor, for effective and sensitive use of both the rapier and the broadsword.

To Angie, for her creativity and dedication, leading to a book cover design that followed my brief meticulously and added her design flair.

To Peter and Kavita, for providing access to insight about a chapter of this book, leading to the possibility of a potential second book for a wider audience.

To Sháá, for her inspiration.

To all those other friends, too numerous to mention individually, who have supported and encouraged me through challenging times and great adversity. I hope I have expressed my gratitude along the way, but know that has never been a resounding strength of mine. I trust it is never too late to thank you from my heart.